THE ETHICS OF AI

THE ETHICS OF AI

FACTS, FICTIONS, AND FORECASTS

ALBERTO CHIERICI

NEW DEGREE PRESS
COPYRIGHT © 2021 ALBERTO CHIERICI
All rights reserved.

THE ETHICS OF AI
Facts, Fictions, and Forecasts

ISBN   978-1-63676-365-1   *Paperback*
        978-1-63676-444-3   *Kindle Ebook*
        978-1-63676-366-8   *Ebook*

To Lallina, for the perseverance, the caring love, and for upgrading my software—love you.

Contents

INTRODUCTION		9
CHAPTER 1.	THE ORIGINS OF AI	21
CHAPTER 2.	WHAT IS ARTIFICIAL INTELLIGENCE	39
CHAPTER 3.	MACHINE AND HUMAN LEARNING	57
CHAPTER 4.	LIMITATIONS OF AI	71
CHAPTER 5.	AI, FROM FICTION TO BEHAVIORAL SCIENCE	89
CHAPTER 6.	CASE STUDIES	109
CHAPTER 7.	WHAT SHOULD AI ETHICS FOCUS ON?	129
CHAPTER 8.	WHAT IS HUMAN: PART I	153
CHAPTER 9.	WHAT IS HUMAN: PART II	165
CHAPTER 10.	ETHICAL AI OR ETHICAL HUMANS?	183
ACKNOWLEDGMENTS		197
APPENDIX		201
ENDNOTES		223

Introduction

I've spent more than ten years working in data science and solving problems at the cross-section of math, algorithmic decision-making, economics, and behavioral science. I've built two companies and helped other entrepreneurs build theirs. These experiences have taught me what it takes to build a business from the ground up and shown me the challenges of trying to make moral decisions in challenging situations.

I felt compelled to write to let these experiences shed an original light on understanding AI and the social, ethical, and cultural implications this technology is already generating. Everyone can start doing two things right now: get educated and open up a respectful, inclusive conversation about morality, truth, and our values.

Call me naive, but I believe that, deep down, we all know right from wrong.

You see, I was taught early on that everyone has a conscience, or inner voice, that helps give them the strength to make tough decisions. This inner voice is the primary source of critical thinking. Sometimes we give it up because of external forces like complacency, fear, or merely a little bit of laziness. It requires discipline, and sometimes hard work, to keep listening to that inner voice. With this book, I want to encourage readers to think critically about reality by providing education first and foremost.

I started my career working as an actuary in London. Actuaries are very similar to modern data scientists. They use statistical models, computer programming, and business skills to predict future outcomes, such as the likelihood of a car crash and how much it's going to cost. The same types of techniques drive prices of health insurance, pension funds, investment plans, and life insurance. So, the step between mathematics to real-world societal impact is quite small when you look at it.

Working as an actuary enabled me to pursue a lifelong enthusiasm for exploring the intersection of economics, risk management, and math. It wasn't long before my career path took a natural turn and landed me in the field of data science. In 2013, I started self-teaching machine learning (ML) and artificial intelligence (AI), the bread-and-butter techniques data scientists use to turn data into useful insights and predictions. The more I learned about such tools, the more I found it entertaining to hear the media narratives on AI and ML. I participated in many conferences during my consulting years, and I was invited to give talks when I started my first company. I was disturbed by some of the questions I was asked. For instance, will AI take over the world? When will AI become more intelligent than humans?

These fears have been perpetuated for the past several decades, leading to sensational and often misleading news headlines like "Alibaba and Microsoft AI Beat Humans in Stanford Reading Test" (Lucas, 2018) and "Artificially Intelligent Painters Invent New Styles of Art" (Baraniuk, 2017). Such publications, seemingly ripped from the pages of a science fiction novel, show how little we understand about artificial intelligence. By the way, this technology isn't even that new. In the late nineties—the period of time known as the "cold winter of AI" because reality deflated the hype generated by the first commercial applications of AI—you could still read articles like "Could a Computer Think like a Human?": the catchy headline of a 1997 opinion piece published in *The Irish Times*.

The leaders of the AI industry and academic research don't exactly help solve this problem, either. Many of them do an excellent job identifying the issues and potential threats AI poses, but they often fail to address these concerns, instead advocating for regulation as the only safety net for consumers.

Many technology, science, and business leaders have voiced concerns about AI. High-caliber scientists like Stephen Hawking, who once said to the *BBC*, "The development of full artificial intelligence could spell the end of the human race.... It would take off on its own and re-design itself at an ever-increasing rate. Humans, who are limited by slow biological evolution, couldn't compete and would be superseded" (Cellan-Jones, 2014).

An even greater authority in the field—the father of modern computing, Alan Turing—said that "it seems probable that once the machine thinking method had started, it would not take long to outstrip our feeble powers ... They would be able to converse with each other to sharpen their wits. At some stage, therefore, we should have to expect the machines to take control" (Turing, 1951).

Technology philosopher and artist Gray Scott highlights the dilemmas of the most advocated solution, regulation, in a famous quote attributed to him: "The real question is, when will we draft an artificial intelligence bill of rights? What will that consist of? And who will get to decide that?" (Marr, 2017).

Who has control is a critical question. Do we trust the elites and politicians governing a state or a society enough to make such a decision? Do they have enough understanding of the technology and the real issues at stake? Moreover, it is important to keep the conversation focused on real, practical matters. For example, futurists arguing for an AI bill of rights should first prove that an engineering artifact made up of several lines of code can be considered at the same level of natural right as a human person!

Regulations are certainly part of the solution, but I want to argue that there is more we can start doing right now.

While many leaders from this field have been spinning their wheels, others agree that the sensational fears they are broadcasting to consumers aren't at all the real threat we should be worried about as AI continues to develop. In fact, there are far more troubling things beneath the surface.

The shift of jobs and its societal impact is one example. A pragmatic voice alerting against near-term issues that AI is causing is Andrew Ng, co-founder of Google Brain, Coursera, and, recently, Deeplearning.ai. Ng points out, "We have seen AI providing conversation and comfort to the lonely; we have also seen AI engaging in racial discrimination. Yet the biggest harm that AI is likely to do to individuals in the short term is job displacement, as the amount of work we can automate with AI is vastly larger than before. As leaders, it is incumbent on all of us to make sure we are building a world in which every individual has an opportunity to thrive" (Ng, 2016).

In a society that seems to be going inevitably toward automating everything, some point out the need for more human values. AI practitioner Amit Ray, author of *Compassionate Artificial Intelligence*, calls for leaders who embrace increasing automation and algorithmic decision-making to be more compassionate: "As more and more artificial intelligence is entering into the world, more and more emotional intelligence must enter into leadership" (Ray, 2018).

One more troubling field is marketing. Learning how professional marketers use psychology to influence behavior opened up a profound realization. Most of the ethical concerns and moral dilemmas that AI applications generate aren't anything new. Most applications of AI that create problems concern the same thing that marketing has always done: influencing behavior. Perhaps more troubling is that, with modern advancements to AI, these programs are getting faster, more efficient, and more accurate.

The issues enumerated above reveal what I believe is the critical issue underneath the creation of an ethical framework for AI and its impact on the future of work and society: the problem of truth.

This point is powerfully made in the recent documentary *The Social Dilemma*, produced by Netflix in 2020. At one point, the film describes how big tech companies profit off of advertising. AI systems power the majority of the algorithms they use for getting people to click more on advertisements: more clicks equals more ad revenue.

In fact, some examples of ethical issues in AI come from the company that embeds AI into everything it does—Google. The company started in 1996, offering its users something truly revolutionary: a search engine that could help them find information better and faster on the internet. Searching is a basic form of a computer science problem that AI techniques solve well enough. It has a simple and practical purpose.

Google was not born with moral dilemmas from the outset. However, once its business model became focused on advertising, engineers started optimizing algorithms for promoting advertisement. This way of making money created new issues on the ethical side. For example, Google-owned YouTube's recommendation algorithms need to increase the time spent viewing in order to grow revenue from advertising.

The algorithms do not account and cannot know whether any information they are pushing to the user's page is true. Their sole objective is to get clicks. That benefits the spread of fake news, which, according to a recent MIT study, spread six times faster on social media than true stories (Dizikes, 2018). As Sandy Parakilas, former operations manager at Uber and product manager at Facebook, says in *The Social Dilemma*, "We've created a system that biases towards false information... because that makes companies more money."

The leading voice and narrator of the documentary is Tristan Harris, one of the most vocal activists exposing serious issues caused by technology companies and AI applications. Once described as the "closest thing Silicon Valley has to a conscience," Harris was a Google design ethicist who is now co-founder and president of the Center for Humane Technology (Bosker, 2016). In the documentary, he says, "If we don't agree on what is true, or that there's such a thing as truth, we are toast! This is the problem beneath other problems because if we don't agree on what's true, then we can't navigate out of any of our problems."

I believe with that sentence, Harris touches a nerve of today's society.

The view of the human person as a mere consumer is perhaps a consequence of the philosophy of relativism, or "the view that truth and falsity, right and wrong, standards of reasoning, and procedures of justification are products of differing conventions and frameworks of assessment and that their authority is confined to the context giving rise to them" (*Stanford Encyclopedia of Philosophy*).

Simply put, people struggle to agree on how to discern right from wrong.

A modern voice that often addresses moral relativism is Pope Francis. His words in *Laudato Si'* help highlight the connection between relativism and the exploitation of modern technology (like AI), which treats human beings as mere profit generators: "When human beings place themselves at the center, they give absolute priority to immediate convenience and all else becomes relative. Hence we should not be surprised to find, in conjunction with the omnipresent technocratic paradigm and the cult of unlimited human power, the rise of a relativism which sees everything as irrelevant unless it serves one's own immediate interests. There is a logic in all this whereby different attitudes can feed on one another, leading to environmental degradation and social decay" (Francis, 2015).

It is important to be realistic when we say artificial intelligence can do X, Y, and Z. Then we shall have the courage to question our beliefs and assumptions deep down: Do we espouse the view that the human person is merely someone through which we create profit? What is the human person, and what is the best way to address the needs of a customer, a child, a parent, a free citizen?

I want to dedicate this book to business leaders and professionals eager for answers, those driving AI adoption at their companies, and the engineers who develop AI solutions for helping them find their inner voice.

While many resources work in silos, this is the first work that links AI education and digestible technical content with psychology, case studies, moral dilemmas, philosophy, and a compass for your own critical thinking.

If you picked up this book, you have a desire to learn. You are looking for original thinking that you can leverage for ethical decision making in your job and in your personal life. You will read about what AI really is, how it is connected with behavioral change, forces that move social trends, and the broader economy.

Artificial Intelligence is a fantastic technology. Many of its promises might be a bit too inflated, but it indeed has the potential to create new opportunities. Armed with education and a commitment to addressing deep questions about truth and meaning, we can decide what products, services, and governance model we shall build for serving the person as a whole, rather than treating people like machines. As with any stepping-stone of human progress, this allows us to step back and reflect on what kind of future we want to build.

> "What intrigues us as a problem, and what will satisfy us as a solution, will depend upon the line we draw between what is already clear and what needs to be clarified."
> —NELSON GOODMAN IN *FACT, FICTION, AND FORECAST*

CHAPTER 1

The Origins of AI

Do technology and progress necessarily improve life?

The often-cited counterexample is the atomic bomb. Physics made big leaps between the nineteen and twentieth centuries. We owe many of the following technological developments to the laws of relativity, quantum mechanics, and semiconductors—all theories that originated back then. Otto Hahn, Lise Meitner, and Fritz Strassman discovered nuclear fission in a laboratory in Berlin, Germany, in 1938 (History.com, 2020). This made the first atomic bomb possible and led to the discovery of an efficient, large-scale source of clean energy.

Going to a less dramatic example, I am a millennial born in the eighties, and I was a teenager between the nineties and early 2000s. The first time I used the internet was around 1997. I remember arguing with friends about Netscape vs. Explorer, downloading music on Napster, and messaging friends on MSN, but that was just a closed circle of geeks. Those tools were not nearly as popular as today's messaging platforms, browsers, and social media platforms.

When I wanted to get together with my friends, we used the so-called telephone chains (or telephone trees). One person was in charge of starting the chain. She would contact two people, who would then contact two people themselves, and so on until all people were contacted. One person decided a time and location, and everyone would meet there. Agreement was reached in a couple of hours, and I would go out the next day, certain I would meet my friends and have a great night. It was beautifully simple.

Today we use WhatsApp groups. Nobody's in charge of starting or setting anything. Some people will start proposing places and times, then others will start debating the day or the time that suits them best. It takes several messages and several hours to finally agree on a place and time, usually several days ahead from the event because syncing up everyone's agenda is like arranging a G8 meeting between prime ministers. A few days ahead of the meet up, we get the usual people trying to sabotage the event. They managed to mix up too many meetups, so they try to rearrange their agendas. Some people get upset and leave the group. Then a few private conversations spin off the group to gossip or talk badly about the saboteurs and whether they should be cut loose. The meetup gets postponed. When the day finally arrives, a few hours before the event, you start getting a few "I'm sorry, I can't make it" messages. A few hours after the agreed time, I would get the occasional "Sorry, I'm a bit late, can you share the location?"

It takes several days, mental strain, and broken friendships just to agree on a night out. Technology and progress don't necessarily improve life.

New means of communication like WhatsApp, in my personal experience, seem to have brought a decrease in "perceived" responsibilities. Too much communication that is free for all makes it hard to commit or make conversations meaningful. While this has not always been the case throughout the history of human development, AI might work in a different way compared to other technological advancements.

Historian Yuval N. Harari makes an interesting argument regarding human progress, or lack thereof. For most of our 2.5 million years as a species, humans had a hunter-gatherer lifestyle. Ten thousand years ago, agriculture altered the course of sapiens' history. Harari explains that this was not progress: "The Agricultural Revolution certainly enlarged the sum total of food at the disposal of humankind, but the extra food did not translate into a better diet or more leisure. Rather, it translated into population explosions and pampered elites. The average farmer worked harder than the average forager and got a worse diet in return" (Harari, 2014).

Agriculture enabled sapiens to grow in number, but at a disastrous cost: less leisure, more work, a more inadequate diet, and apparently shorter lifespans.

An agricultural civilization also meant switching from a nomadic lifestyle to settling down into defined areas for the long term. So, we started clearing forests, diverting streams, growing crops, taming animals, and building permanent structures. These activities and systems fathered the need for more complex social and organizational networks, paving the way for cities, states, and eventually empires.

Unfortunately, the unpretentious farmer had to abdicate much of his surplus yield to the rulers, who often ran nothing more than extortion rackets. Harari concludes, "This is the essence of the Agricultural Revolution: the ability to keep more people alive under worse conditions."

While Harari runs over many oversimplifications (which is expected for a history of Homo sapiens in just above four hundred pages) and does not present any evidence that hunter-gather societies were happier than rural ones, he points out an interesting concept: significant historical changes and revolution—big and small—may sometimes worsen the human condition.

AI is often described as a revolutionary technology, something that will change many things. As we will see later, there are some overstatements and some truths to that. What I want to underline at this point is that we're still in a historical moment where we can step back and reflect on how we want to develop this technology further. And we definitely don't want to end up worse off.

Let's start by first appreciating where AI comes from by showing how AI developed at the crossroads of many disciplines. The fundamental disciplines and processes that culminated into AI include philosophy, mathematics, economics, neuroscience, psychology, computer engineering, control theory, cybernetics, and linguistics.

THE MULTIDISCIPLINARY ORIGIN OF AI

The foundations of artificial intelligence can be traced back many centuries, beginning with ancient philosophers.

The Greek philosopher Aristotle (384–322 BC) formulated the laws that govern the human mind's rational side. His system of syllogism consisted of providing a way to generate conclusions mechanically, given initial premises. An example of syllogism would be, "All cars have wheels. I drive a car. Therefore, my car has wheels."

The field of philosophy influenced AI's birth by tackling questions like the relationship between the brain and the mind, thinking, knowledge, and the relationship between knowledge and action. We'll discuss in later chapters how philosophy is still influential today, especially when it comes to moral decision-making.

The critical influence of Aristotle's philosophy was that if good reasoning shall follow logical and mechanical laws, it can be replicated by an engineering artifact.

Fast-forward to the fifteenth century, where the French philosopher René Descartes (1596–1650) was the most important figure for understanding the original principles of modern scientific thinking. He was the first to formalize the distinction between mind and matter.

A few problems arise from this conception of the world. Stuart Russell and Peter Norvig, in their classic computer science textbook *Artificial Intelligence: A Modern Approach*, explain that a purely physical conception of the mind leaves little room for free will. If the human mind behaves logically and mechanically like an Aristotelian syllogism, every decision is an automated deduction. Free will would be just a perception of the way the available choice appears to the choosing entity.

It is worth noting that Descartes was also a proponent of "dualism": the notion that there is a part of the human mind (or soul or spirit) that is outside of nature, exempt from physical laws. Animals, on the other hand, did not possess this dual quality; they could be treated as machines. This view culminated with evolutionary thinking developing a few centuries later: humans were considered no different than animals (Beckermann, 2010). Consequently, humans too could be treated like machines.

Walking through history toward the Modern Age, we see how mathematics, economics, and many other modern sciences contributed to the field.

Mathematics gave to AI formal rules to drive conclusions, defining what can be computed. Statistics, a branch of mathematics, formalized reasoning and developed more precise methods for calculating what we can discern from uncertain information. Statistics was particularly influential in modern AI. In fact, most of the techniques known as machine learning have a statistical foundation, as you'll learn later on.

Economics investigates problems like decision-making for maximizing payoff, what to do when there are multiple stakeholders maximizing different values, and what happens when these objectives materialize in long timeframes. The science of economics started in 1776, when Scottish philosopher Adam Smith (1723–1790) published *An Inquiry into the Nature and Causes of the Wealth of Nations*. Smith was the first to treat the subject as a science, using the idea that economies can be thought of as individual agents maximizing their own economic well-being.

Smith's view of economics is still the most influential among mainstream economists. Some argue its limited definition of what a human person is stands at the root of many problems we have today regarding how companies operate. Focusing on tech companies using AI has a dramatic impact, as we'll see later.

Neuroscience, the study of the nervous system, particularly the brain, studies how brains process information and inspired modern AI computational approaches like neural networks.

Psychology studies how humans and animals think and act. There have been mutual influences between psychology and computer science involving the same academics who are considered the fathers of AI and who started the field of cognitive science at MIT in the 1950s. Today, a common (although far from universal) view among psychologists is that "a cognitive theory should be like a computer program" (Anderson, 1980). The recent development of behavioral science has influenced how modern AI products are being developed by big tech firms and modern startups.

Fields related to engineering and language complete the spectrum of influencers for the AI field. For artificial intelligence to succeed, we need two things: intelligence and an engineering artifact. The computer has been the best candidate for the artifact. Building increasingly efficient computers is a crucial part of developing AI. As a branch of computer science, AI itself influenced how to construct efficient machines. Control theory and cybernetics studies how engineering artifacts can operate on their own. Linguistics studies how language relates to thought. Modern linguistics and AI were "born" at about the same time. They grew up together, intersecting in a hybrid field called computational linguistics, or natural language processing.

THE FIRST TIME WE HEARD OF "ARTIFICIAL INTELLIGENCE"

The official birth of AI is pinpointed in a Dartmouth workshop in summer 1956. This was the first time that John McCarthy's term *artificial intelligence* was officially used. McCarthy, after receiving his PhD from Princeton in 1951 and working for two years as an instructor, moved to Stanford and then to Dartmouth College. He then convinced other influential mathematicians and computer scientists, Marvin Minsky, Claude Shannon, and Nathaniel Rochester, to bring together US researchers interested in automata theory, neural networks, and the study of intelligence.

They organized a two-month workshop at Dartmouth in the summer of 1956. The proposal stated:

> We propose that a two-month, ten-man study of artificial intelligence be carried out during the summer of 1956 at Dartmouth College in Hanover, New Hampshire. The study is to proceed on the basis of

the conjecture that every aspect of learning or any other feature of intelligence can in principle be so precisely described that a machine can be made to simulate it. An attempt will be made to find how to make machines use language, form abstractions, and concepts, solve kinds of problems now reserved for humans, and improve themselves. We think that a significant advance can be made in one or more of these problems if a carefully selected group of scientists work on it together for a summer.

The Dartmouth workshop did not lead to any new breakthroughs. Still, it did introduce all the significant figures to each other. For the next twenty years, the field would be dominated by these people and their students and colleagues at the Massachusetts Institute of Technology, Carnegie Mellon, Stanford, and International Business Machines (IBM).

The development of computing, the internet, software applications, operating systems, mobile devices, and wearables built upon AI's success in specific tasks such as recognizing patterns, images, and speech. As a feedback loop, widespread usage of such tools and the availability of massive data sources reinforced the success of these specific applications of AI.

Despite these successes, though, some influential founders of AI, including McCarthy, Minsky, Nils Nilsson, and Patrick Winston, didn't seem to be happy with the progress of AI, according to Russell and Norvig. They thought that AI should put less emphasis on creating ever-improved versions of applications that are good at a specific task. Instead, they believed AI should return to its roots of striving for "machines that think, that learn, and that create." They call the effort human-level AI, or HLAI. Similarly, some AI figures formulated the idea of artificial general intelligence, or AGI. AGI looks for a universal algorithm for learning and acting in any environment and has its roots in Ray Solomonoff's work, one of the attendees of the original 1956 Dartmouth conference (Russell and Norvig, 2013).

Though fascinating, it is debatable whether or not the "purist" academic endeavor of creating artificial general intelligence is possible to achieve. Some labs still exist and were recently founded with that purpose. Eventually, some large tech companies buy them and use their resources for achieving business objectives. AGI quests tend to be short-lived, focusing on short-term applications that solve specific tasks. A notable example is Deep Mind, the London lab born with the quest for solving AGI. While it is allegedly reported to work on long-term health care and science problems, it is unclear to what extent commercial objectives replaced its original aim (Hodson, 2019).

Today's AI history is undoubtedly connected with and influenced by economic development.

AI MEETS CAPITAL

Like many technological breakthroughs, AI was initially a philosophical and scientific endeavor until it became an economic propellant between the 1980s and the early twenty-first century.

The first successful commercial applications of AI took the form of the so-called *expert systems*. These are programs where knowledge is hardcoded into a set of rules from textbooks, direct experience, and interviewing a large number of subject matter experts. Each rule codifies a level of certainty for its specific application. The system would then use probability to compute the most likely knowledge item for a new scenario.

One of the first expert systems developed was in the area of medical diagnosis (Russell and Norvig, 2013). MYCIN was developed over five to six years in the early 1970s at Stanford University for diagnosing blood infections. Its creators hard-coded about 450 rules. The system performed as well as some experts, and considerably better than junior doctors. Despite its performance and strengths, MYCIN was never used in practice because, at the time, the state of technologies for integrating the system with existing tools was underdeveloped. Moreover, some observers raised ethical and legal issues related to the use of computers in medicine.

This new, robust automation level became an industry in the 1980s with the first commercially successful expert system, R1, deployed at the Digital Equipment Corporation. The program helped configure orders for new computer systems. It was saving the company about $40 million a year by 1986. Two years later, DEC's AI group deployed forty expert systems and had more on the way. DuPont had one hundred in use and five hundred in development, saving an estimated $10 million a year. Nearly every major US corporation had its own AI group and was either using or investigating expert systems.

The commercial success of AI drove forward research and investment in R&D. Hundreds of companies were created in the fields of robotics, vision, language processing, and software to support such applications. In the 1990s, there was an "AI winter" that occurred parallel to the internet's development and culminated with the dot-com bubble. These companies didn't live up to their hype and promises. At the same time, too much capital and exuberance kept flowing into these businesses.

The lesson here is that commercial AI, like many other technologies, was developed and built mainly to satisfy economic goals. The expert systems created considerable savings for businesses. Still, we had to wait for the personal computer's maturity and the omnipresence of the internet (that smartphone and wearable devices brought in the first decade of the twenty-first century) to see a second explosion in AI adoption.

This time, the main force of development was data, capital, and socially engineered trends.

AI not only helped cut costs and increase productivity—this technology was directly responsible for hyper-growing user numbers, revenues, and companies' valuations. This was the ideal type of business for venture capital firms to target: companies that can grow ten or twenty times in less than ten years.

Google search is a direct application of AI. Artificial intelligence techniques are responsible for making the search algorithm work better and faster. The better the algorithm worked, the more users it got.

Facebook, LinkedIn, and other social networks use AI to suggest connections, hence expanding the network and the user base.

Amazon, Spotify, and Netflix use recommendation algorithms (developed using AI techniques) to increase sales, usage, and hours of listening and watching.

It's no wonder the majority of these internet companies have as their core an ad-based business model. They offer a product that is free to use, and they make money by selling the best display space for promoters.

A platform that uses AI to capture hours and hours of people's time gathers people's attention span and a lot of valuable data. Brands, in turn, can use AI techniques themselves for hyper-targeting their ads. Tristan Harris calls this economic development "the attention economy" in the documentary *The Social Dilemma* (Orlowski, 2020).

The economy is as widely intertwined with the development of AI as the moral problem is. Speaking about moral decision-making in the field of AI and paving a framework for its ethical development cannot be detached from a reflection about how our economy works and how we want to design it for the future.

MACROECONOMIC TRENDS AND MORAL QUESTIONS
Esteemed Italian economist and banker Ettore Gotti Tedeschi, ex-president of the Vatican Bank and current Chairman at Santander Consumer Bank SpA, noted three crucial economic

trends. First, work is changing. Second, the economic development model will change. Third, companies will necessarily adapt to the first two changes (Russo and Vaccaro, 2013).

Why is work changing? There are far too many unemployed people in the world—about two hundred million (O'Neill, 2021). Surprisingly, forty million are in developed countries. Gotti Tedeschi explains how this tragic outcome came about. When the rich and developed world decides to slow down births, it has to start two processes for getting the GDP (gross domestic product) growth back on track. One is to increase productivity (for example, via technology innovation). One is delocalizing production in cheap labor countries (for increasing consumption at a lower cost). Lastly, financing consumption using debt viciously accelerates the first two processes. The hope is to make up for the growth of the debt that funded consumption in the first place while compensating the fixed costs due to the aging of the population (and the consequent higher taxation for supporting the elderly). One more consequence is sacrificing savings for consumerism.

The process described above accelerates the displacement of production toward countries where labor is cheap, thus creating jobs in the poorer countries and increasing unemployment in the richer countries. The economic crisis explodes when the debt issued for financing the consumerism that's necessary for growing becomes unsustainable. It then causes the crash of consumption itself as well as production, employment, and so forth in a domino effect.

Unfortunately, returning to full employment will be problematic in developed countries because it requires considerable investments in technological innovation and a radical change in lifestyle and work life.

According to Gotti Tedeschi, the development model will change because, in the past thirty years, we have created a new world economic order. We split the world into two: producing countries (China, for example) and consuming countries that are increasingly less often producers (the West). We've eventually impoverished the West and put it at risk because it's now too dependent on the producing countries, and Western people are more reluctant to do production and manufacturing jobs.

We saw that commercial AI developed to meet economic goals. If an economic objective is not moral in itself, then the technology which enables the objective cannot be blamed. It is the goal that should change.

Thus, Gotti Tedeschi asks if it is possible to get out of the economic crisis he described without addressing the moral objective. His answer is a clear no, and he goes on by suggesting that we shall reconsider the meaning of financial profit, how and what we define as success, and how we develop a more humane economy.

I sympathize with Gotti Tedeschi's conclusion. I don't believe there are technical solutions, like a different economic indicator to optimize, a new set of regulations, or political agreements between nations that can solve what seems to be a problem of human morality.

We cannot keep avoiding key moral questions: Is it right or wrong to outsource work to cheap labor countries? Is it right or wrong to keep promoting practices that reduce births? Is it right or wrong to reward success at work with huge bonuses? Is it right or wrong to close an eye to environmental pollution in order to maximize profits? This list of questions could go on for a while. The point is that we shall bring the debate to a moral level rather than sticking to the surface-level technicalities.

I'll revisit these questions and the moral and philosophical frameworks that can help with diving into them in later chapters. I began this chapter by asking if every technological progression brings humans to be better off. AI is a fascinating quest that originated in ancient times and combined multiple disciplines. It became a real thing only in recent years thanks to scientific and technological advances. While it seems that many technologies have not yet been shown to directly benefit humankind, can AI diverge from the norm? It is time to learn what AI actually is and what real-world applications are behind the hype.

Artificial:
"*While* artificial *can simply mean 'made by humans,' it's often used in a negative sense, conveying the idea that an artificial product is inferior to the real thing. If you remark that your friend's new hair color looks artificial, for example, you're not paying her a compliment.* Artificial *can also describe a behavior or expression that seems insincere—much like the smile on your girlfriend's face if you bring her artificial flowers instead of real ones.*"

—VOCABULARY.COM

Intelligence:
"*(1) the ability to learn or understand or to deal with new or trying situations: REASON*

also: the skilled use of reason;

(2): the ability to apply knowledge to manipulate one's environment or to think abstractly as measured by objective criteria (such as tests)."

—MERRIAM-WEBSTER VOCABULARY

CHAPTER 2

What Is Artificial Intelligence

I first heard the term "artificial intelligence" in 1999. Though I was only fourteen, I remember that day vividly. My dad and I had gone out to the local cinema to watch *The Matrix*.

Though I didn't know it at the time, that movie would change my life forever. Within the first five minutes of the film, my heart was racing through the fight scenes that introduced that amazing 360-degree, slow-motion camera view of cool kung fu moves. The cinema sat above a metro station, and trains passing by made the floor and seats vibrate a little, which added a fantastic vibe to the lines of *The Matrix's* code scrolling over the screen. On our way back home, I could tell how incredibly energized my dad, a lifelong science fiction fan, was by the way he was riding (or racing?) the motorbike. I was also jazzed by the movie (and my dad's sporty driving)!

Action movies and science fiction took a leap that would define cinematography forever. As a matter of fact, twenty years later, I have to say the impression was confirmed. I now realize that the film has also influenced the public's understanding of AI, as well as my nascent passion with computers and internet technologies.

The Matrix, like many other movies about robotics and artificial intelligence I would watch in my youth, made AI cool and fascinating. The movie introduced fantastic themes about technology, power, control, and the relationship between humans and machines—which we'll explore later—but it also gave me a misinformed understanding of this field.

While we're accustomed to the fictions of AI, I want to present the facts. Starting from the public perception of AI, we'll move to factual definitions.

WHAT PEOPLE THINK AI IS

Robotics companies, movies, and the media often exaggerate AI and its capabilities. For example, a thought-provoking article in *Futurism* describes a robot's demo, Sophia, who can interact with a human interrogator in a seemingly natural way. It can also smile and mirror facial expressions that are common to humans to the extent that the CEO of the company that created it said, "Oh yeah, she's basically alive" (Robitzski, 2018).

When the public sees such demonstrations, it's easy to be tricked into thinking that we already have the robots we have seen in science fiction movies, from the century-old *Metropolis* to the more recent thriller *Ex Machina*. In fact, even experts in the field have fallen prey to the superstitions of science fiction.

Elon Musk, SpaceX founder and Tesla CEO, reportedly spoke about AI being humanity's greatest existential threat. In a 2014 interview at MIT, he said:

"I think we should be very careful about artificial intelligence. If I had to guess what our biggest existential threat is, it's probably that . . . I'm increasingly inclined to think that there should be some regulatory oversight, maybe at the national and international level, just to make sure that we don't do something very foolish" (MIT AeroAstro, 2014).

Tesla is a pioneer of self-driving cars, a technology developed using AI techniques. In fact, Musk can say with confidence "that we're headed toward a situation where AI is vastly smarter than humans, and I think that time frame is less than five years from now. But that doesn't mean that everything goes to hell in five years. It just means that things get unstable or weird" (Dowd, 2020).

A quick search for news about AI reveals how the press speaks about this technology. When you read headlines such as "We Are Still Smarter than Computers. For Now" (Ovide, 2020), or "Police Drones Are Starting to Think for Themselves" (Metz, 2020), you may think that AI is a technology so powerful that it makes computers able to think and act autonomously.

Nancy Fulda, a computer scientist working on broader AI systems at Brigham Young University, told *Futurism*, "I am frequently entertained to see the way my research takes on exaggerated proportions as it progresses through the media. The whole thing is a bit like a game of 'telephone'—the technical details of the project get lost, and the system begins to seem self-willed and almost magical. At some point, I almost don't recognize my own research anymore" (Robitzski, 2018).

In a 2020 interview with Maureen Dowd, Elon Musk said he believes "AI is overlooked by very smart people [because] very smart people do not think a computer can ever be as smart as they are." Musk's worries about AI are not entirely misplaced, but they also fail to see the bigger picture. Experts in the field of AI often contradict Musk's assertion, not because they *think* they know better, but because they actually do.

As we make progress in this field, it's crucial that we help the public understand what this technology is in actuality in order to help them see the more practical consequences it generates. Let's start with where AI is currently being used.

REAL-WORLD AI APPLICATIONS

While *The Matrix* may have given me unrealistic expectations of what AI was and could do, it also inspired me to want to learn more. Since that day, I've made it my mission to learn everything I could about this field wherever I could—in university, at work, or in my own free time. While I was still a teenager, it was naively using computers and understanding programs. I always dismissed coding classes, both in high school and at the undergraduate level (what a big mistake!).

I was more into the hardware and using those new, magic tools until the day came when I could no longer escape the world of computer science. Ironically, I ended up enrolling into a PhD program on the subject late in life.

One course I found that helped me understand the computer science aspect of AI was from Columbia University. I got to work in 2014 by registering for a class, provided free-of-charge by online learning platform EdX (Salleb-Aouissi, 2014). In one of the first lessons, I learned about the search problem.

Searching is a cornerstone problem in computer science. It is used for designing algorithms, data structures, and optimizing speed and physical memory used by a computer. Search is one of the problems to which AI brought a practical solution. It's not by chance that the company at the forefront of AI development today is Google. This business started as a search engine.

From my years of professional work and research in this field, I've learned that AI is all around us, influencing our day-to-day digital interactions in ways we may not even fully understand.

Many of the apps you might use every day, like Apple News, Facebook, Twitter, YouTube, Netflix, Amazon, or Spotify, often filter the news and posts you may be more interested in reading. They also recommend the next video or movie you should watch, the next item you should buy, or the next song they think you'll want to hear. Their recommendations aren't random—in fact, they always feel spot on. How do they do that? They use AI.

Several mainstream news' sites now offer personalized content to paid subscribers based on their interests. For instance, *The New York Times'* home page you're looking at in your browser now may look very different from the one I see at the same time, while the printed version is the same for all readers. Computer algorithms determine pictures and content to show us based on our location, browsing history, and website activity, which includes clicks and time spent on a page. These algorithms are again a form of AI.

Such systems are a double-edged sword. On one side, they personalize content to make them more convenient and useful to you. Think about Twitter—could you possibly be interested in every single post made by the people you follow or even have the time to read them all? You need some sort of filter, and if the filter is smart enough to figure out what you like, it saves you time. On the other side, though, these companies use personalized content to keep you sticking to the platform. Netflix, Facebook, and YouTube are a few of the companies that aim to increase your time watching or interacting with your social network.

Guillaume Chaslot, a former Google software engineer who worked on the YouTube video recommendation algorithm, said to *The Guardian*, "Watch time was the priority, everything else was considered a distraction" (Lewis, 2018). This was also confirmed in an academic paper written by Google engineers where they describe the impressive improvement achieved by deep neural networks on YouTube recommendations. The authors state, "Our goal is to predict expected watch time" (Covington et al., 2016). A similar technique boosted the Twitter timeline algorithm; this system ranks which tweets you get to see first, as Twitter engineers Koumchatzky and Andryeyev (2017) explain in a blog post. In the same blog post, you could see which metrics are most important for the business: "Online experiments have also shown significant increases in metrics such as tweet engagement and time spent on the platform. And as we've shared before during our previous earnings, the updated timeline has in part driven increases in both audience and engagement on Twitter."

While this may seem convenient to the average, everyday user, there are often unintended (and sadly, sometimes intended) consequences when AI is used to personalize content. Filter bubbles, echo chambers, and troll factories can develop, and, if left unchecked, become a dangerous environment for hate and misinformation (Pierre, 2016). To understand how these unintended consequences may happen, we shall first define what AI is and what it is not.

DEFINING AI

I recently took a career break and decided to pursue a doctorate in computer science at New York University Abu Dhabi. As part of the program, I spent a year in New York City taking classes. During my time in New York, I took an unforgettable class: "Responsible Data Science" taught by Julia Stoyanovich, assistant professor in the department of computer science and engineering at the Tandon School of Engineering, and the Center for Data Science. In the class, I learned about many of the ideas I eventually decided to develop in this book. After that experience, I did volunteer work for a cultural event in the city, scheduled in February

2020. I led a group of data science professionals and young academics across the US, creating an exhibition on AI for the general public. We wanted to educate visitors about AI and understanding its social impact.

While preparing it, we faced the problem of explaining difficult, technical concepts to the everyday layperson. We turned to Prof. Stoyanovich, who suggested looking at the University of Helsinki's free online course, "Elements of AI."

"Elements of AI" is a fantastic resource for understanding AI building blocks. It goes through an easy, pragmatic approach to define and explain key concepts of AI, building blocks like machine learning and neural networks, and shows real-world applications of AI as well as its societal implications. This course, and the classic academic textbook used in almost all computer science AI classes (Russell and Norvig, 2013), will be my source of inspiration for the following definitions.

There is a funny definition of AI among geeks. It says that AI is "all cool things that computers cannot do."

The irony behind this definition is that as soon as we find a way to do something cool with a computer, it stops being an AI problem. For example, searching was a difficult problem for computers to solve. It was considered a task that AI could accomplish. Today, nobody really considers searching as an AI task. In a sense, it is correct that it's no longer a "problem" because there is a solution. The solution is, in fact, a system of AI algorithms. Google's search engine uses multiple algorithms from the AI world: natural language processing, retrieval, and ranking are a few of them.

ADAPTABILITY AND AUTONOMY

"Elements of AI" defines AI by highlighting two characteristics.

The first one is autonomy, namely, performing tasks in complex environments without constant user guidance.

The second one is adaptivity, which is the ability to improve performance by acquiring experience.

Let's look at a couple of notorious AI applications: self-driving cars and Spotify's recommendation engine.

Are they autonomous? Certainly yes. An autonomous vehicle can speed, brake, turn, change lanes, and stop at a red signal without constant intervention by a pilot. Spotify doesn't have an army of employees continually checking what you've listened to in order to make recommendations. A computer program suggests a song without constant intervention from someone.

Do they adapt to new environments? In other words, do they perform better by gaining "experience"? While a self-driving car should achieve a performance level near perfect before being deployed on the roads, we can say that it can adapt. Before you can use it, the vehicle's computer programs go through a phase named "training" and field testing. They are fed by enormous amounts of data while being deployed in testing environments. These are controlled and safe areas where the car can move around and acquire more data using various sensors. The more data, or "experience," they get, the more they achieve the level of accuracy necessary for deployment in production environments (the real world). Similarly, Spotify algorithms get better the more you use

Spotify. Suppose you accept (play a suggested song) or reject (ignore a proposed piece). In that case, your decision becomes experience, i.e., an additional data point fed into the computer program. The more you tell Spotify what you like, the more relevant its music recommendations will be.

Historically, AI was defined in many different ways, until these myriad conceptions culminated into the classic definition that Russell and Norvig give in their textbook.

RATIONAL AGENTS

Russell and Norvig organize the way academics approached AI along two dimensions (Figure 1): One is *what* activity a computer program or a robot performs, thinking or acting. The other is *how* the machine or the software behaves, mimicking a human being or following a rational objective.

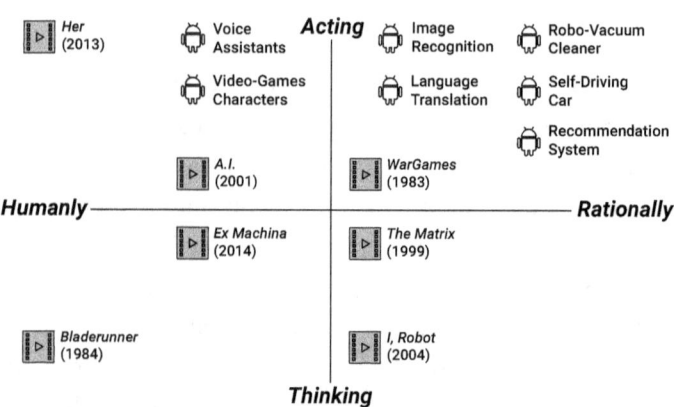

Figure 1: Russell and Norvig's (2013) four quadrants of AI and popular movies vs. real applications.

This model helps us understand how advanced artificial intelligence is by putting it in comparison with human behavior. The axis of this graph distinguishes the differences between a simple pre-programmed action and "thinking."

So, there were four approaches to AI:

1. **Thinking humanly** would include "activities that we associate with human thinking, activities such as decision-making, problem-solving, learning . . ." according to AI pioneer Bellman in 1978.
2. **Thinking rationally** means studying "the computations that make it possible to perceive, reason, and act" in the words of AI pioneer Winston in 1992.
3. Another AI pioneer, Kurzweil, described AI as **acting humanly** in 1990: "the art of creating machines that perform functions that require intelligence when performed by people."
4. **Acting rationally** is what AI engineers learn in computer science degree courses and what they do in the real world: "AI . . . is concerned with intelligent behavior in artifacts" (Nilsson, 1998).

Russel and Norvig point out that:

"The rational-agent approach has two advantages over the other approaches. First, it is more general than the 'laws of thought' approach because correct inference is just one of several possible mechanisms for achieving rationality. Second, it is more amenable to scientific development than are approaches based on human behavior or human thought. The standard of rationality is mathematically well defined and completely general, and can be 'unpacked' to generate agent designs that provably achieve it. Human behavior, on the other hand, is well adapted for one specific environment and is defined by, well, the sum total of all the things that humans do." (Russell and Norvig, 2013)

Given this "four quadrants" framework for categorizing how AI can be approached or defined, it is useful to make a reality check and see which quadrant best describes real-world applications of AI

Most films depict machines or robots that can "think," either humanly or rationally, or computers that act humanly. Movies do this because the sensation sells. It's fear mongering, but it's also intriguing. People want to learn more, but what they're learning from may be misleading them. While science fiction is indeed a source of inspiration for scientists and entrepreneurs alike, AI's real-world applications fall uniquely in a narrow corner of the two-dimensional spectrum. The realm of acting rationally.

Science fiction's role remains essential in science, and there is research supporting it. According to *MIT Technology Review* (2018), a research study from Philipp Jordan, at the University of Hawaii, and a few colleagues "found that researchers use science fiction in a variety of different ways. One is for theoretical design research. Another is to refer to and explore new forms of human-computer interaction, which researchers increasingly think is shaped by science fiction books and films."

Still, we need to detach a little bit from it to better understand what AI is.

The artificial art of flying was achieved by studying air pressure and engineering turbines rather than mimicking how birds fly. Likewise, a self-driving car does not "learn" how to drive by copying how humans operate. Instead, it performs an action following a rational system of rules that are the output of several machine learning and classical computation programs. A recommendation system is a software that performs an action (say, recommends a book) by optimizing a rational objective (increase sales/upsell other books). It doesn't necessarily "think" about what users could like or act like your trusted librarian. It doesn't know you like a human could.

If you still think the automated ads that pop up while you're browsing the internet are a *little* too advanced to be simply based on algorithms, take a look at image recognition. Computer programs that recognize objects in pictures or from a camera's live feed don't reason about, or "see," images like humans. They implement a technique called machine learning that reads many numbers describing color and pixel positions and figures out what object they represent. It can categorize an image as "cat" or "dog" by achieving a set objective (in machine learning jargon, minimizing a loss function).

The machine learning program doesn't know what a cat is or what a dog is. In fact, a notorious study from Ribeiro et al. (2016) reveals what a machine learning algorithm "understood" when it was instructed to classify wolves and huskies. The research paper focused on the use of LIME (a software tool I'll refer to later) to visualize why a husky was classified as a wolf. It turns out that the snow in the image was used to classify the picture as "wolf," meaning that the computer program learned to detect snow rather than huskies in reality!

Despite the attempts to humanize computers, AI remains an engineering tool.

ENGINEERING ARTIFACT

I opened up this chapter by citing dictionary definitions of the words "artificial" and "intelligence." And I'd like to stress that the former comes before the latter. Artificial comes from the Latin words "Ars, Artis (-ium)"—art—and the Latin verb "facio, facere"—to do or make. These words are the same root of the word *artifact*.

As we have seen in the headline examples I mentioned, the word "intelligence" often takes all the credit. Press and marketing speak about machines with human-quality cognitive and intelligent abilities like thinking, learning, and understanding.

The reason why we come across some words like machine "learning," or "understanding" or "intelligence" is mostly because we had the legacy of science fiction, sensational marketing, and corporate propaganda. Perhaps we lack the language to accurately talk about machines because this is how humans understand and describe these processes. So, we unknowingly personify technology by giving it human traits or actions as it's the closest we can come to describing what is actually happening.

Terms like learning, understanding, intelligence have many problems, and they can be misleading. One may well say, for example, that a system has intelligence because it delivers accurate navigation instructions or detects signs of melanoma in spectroscopy images. When we hear something like this, the word "intelligence" suggests that the system can perform a task an intelligent person can accomplish. But would the same systems be able to go to the grocery store and cook dinner?

The adaptability and autonomy of AI may call for a comparison with human behavior or intelligence because humans are adaptable and autonomous. However, we shall look at these terms merely for their utility: if we develop robots and computer programs that need constant human supervision for adapting to new circumstances and could not work on their own, it wouldn't be that much more useful or any different than employing a person for the task.

Finally, the word "intelligence" is not a single dimension, like length or speed. It's not measurable, unlike what people often believe. As scientists, we know that there is no set way for *how* to measure intelligence, or *what* should be measured when trying to make this determination.

Despite this poor choice of words, "artificial intelligence" is not "artificial humanity." We are not talking about an intelligent creature. It is not a creation like the romantic monster of Victor Frankenstein.

AI is an *engineering artifact* that can solve problems and complete tasks *rationally*, with a high degree of *autonomy* and *adaptability*.

As I will thoroughly present later, I reject to view AI as some sort of "intelligent" being. It cannot "think" for itself. Even in the future, it will not enslave humanity unless we prefer being governed by engineering artifacts instead of people.

Machine:
"A mechanically, electrically, or electronically operated device for performing a task."

To learn:
"To gain knowledge or understanding of or skill in by study, instruction, or experience."

—MERRIAM WEBSTER VOCABULARY

CHAPTER 3

Machine and Human Learning

My daughter is almost four years old. Not too long ago, she walked up to me while I was grilling and asked me a question.

"Daddy, what is this?"

— "It's pieces of wood in a bowl of water."

"Why did you do that?"

— "I want to get some smoke in the barbeque."

"How do you make smoke?"

— "You know, if you place wet wood on top of the charcoal, it makes a nice smelling smoke!"

"Ha," she noted, matter-of-factly.

As it is custom with children that age, she asks me an incredible amount of questions. All discussions end with her brief, dry "Ha"—her way to say, "Got it. I understand now."

It fascinates me that she never questions whether my answer makes sense or not. She just accepts things as they are. It's that simple.

With adults, things are never this easy. We are used to reasoning, deducing, or "fact-checking" everything. My daughter does not fact-check everything I say to her. She didn't need to put the wet wood on the barbeque to know how the smoke comes about. She just trusted me.

If I look back at my own experience, most things I learned in life came through a similar process. I didn't need to fact-check or run an experiment to know that America exists. I trusted my primary school teacher, who told me about America and the author of the world map we had on the glass wall. When I learned multiplication tables and basic math, I didn't ask about their inner workings—I just trusted the teachers who taught me that $2 + 2 = 4$. Trust, or "by authority," is one of the most basic ways through which humans learn.

There are many ways humans learn, and the humanity of this style keeps surprising scientists and humanists alike. When speaking of machine learning, we shall be cautious not to assume that machines learn in the same way.

MACHINE LEARNING

Sometimes, AI and ML are even used interchangeably because ML is the way in which AI systems "learn" to accomplish a task.

As we have seen for the term "artificial intelligence," the language we use to describe technological advances is often centered on the human experience, so, as a consequence, it tends to lend human qualities to inhuman objects. This is no different with the term "machine learning." While learning might be the closest we can come up to describing how machines acquire knowledge, this unknowing personification leads us to believe technology can advance beyond us, become autonomous of its creators, and eventually take over the world.

Now, what does machine learning actually mean? And how does it work?

Nowadays, machine learning is the main field of technology that powers most artificial intelligence applications. Building on the definitions given in the previous Chapter, ML is how we humans instruct computers to function as *rational agents* with a certain degree of *autonomy* and *adaptability*.

Machine learning can either be seen as a mathematical and statistical model used to predict a certain outcome, or as a computer programming technique that differs from classical programming (Figure 1).

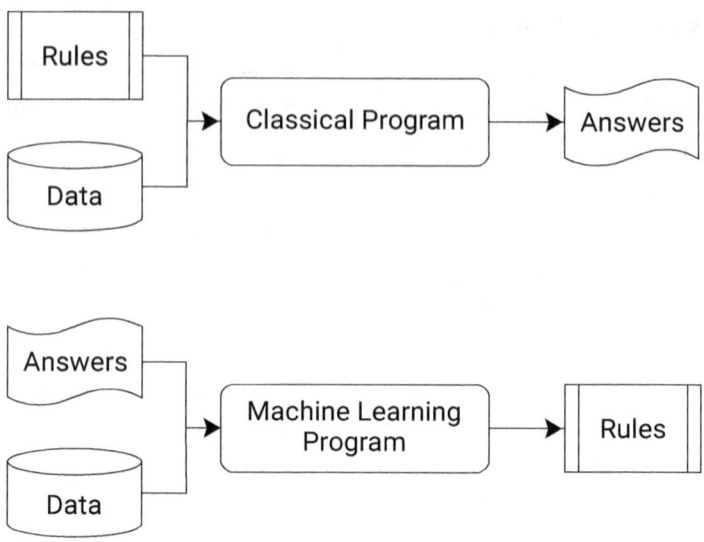

Figure 1: Classical Programming vs. Machine Learning

A classical computer program takes in a mix of rules and data points given to the machine by a programmer and gives you an answer. Think about your calculator. You input data: 2+2, and in return it compiles the input with pre-programmed mathematical rules and gives you an answer: four. It will do this with any set of numbers and symbols you type in, following the rules it was programmed to adhere to.

A machine learning program works differently. It takes data points and answers as input and it outputs rules. Using the same examples, say we want to program a calculator using machine learning. We would input many examples of mathematical operations (data) with their answers. For example, we would input "2 + 2 = 4," "3 x 2 = 6," "10 - 3 = 7," etc. It would need millions of such examples. The program's output is a set of rules to follow for reproducing results similar to the examples it has seen. So, when you input "2 + 2," it should reproduce the example that is as close as possible to the actual mathematical operation: "2 + 2 = 4." Programming a calculator with machine learning is overkill, as in this context it is simple enough to give clear rules to the device.

Moreover, the objective of the calculator is to give the right answer all the time. Machine learning uses statistical techniques and may have a percentage of error. Even if the chance is tiny, a calculator cannot afford to get one answer wrong.

An interesting note here is that ML is known by different names in different fields: *statistical learning* and *pattern recognition* are a couple of examples. The computer program recognizes patterns using statistics. Using the ML-programmed calculator above and machine learning techniques, after seeing tons of times that 2 + 2 = 4, its rules work out a higher probability that the input "2 + 2" should give an output of four, with a lower chance that it equals any other number. How we collect data plays a very important role: if the data isn't enough or overrepresents certain answers over others, the ML program will learn from skewed data in such a way that it is more likely to give you the wrong answer.

Machine learning comes up with rules by combining mathematical, statistical, and computer programming techniques to find data patterns, and this is one reason why engineers describe the method as "learning." Given millions of examples, the program "learns" rules to reproduce such samples.

There are different ways machine learning models discover patterns in data. The three main categories of ML are "supervised," "unsupervised," and "reinforcement" (The University of Helsinki, 2020). The best way to program an application depends on the problem at hand and data availability.

The calculator system described above is an example of supervised learning. We are given inputs with their correct outputs as data examples (the complete equations "2 + 2 = 4," "3 x 2 = 6," "10 - 3 = 7," etc.). The task of the machine is to learn how to reproduce the correct result of an equation. The results of the equations in the data input are called "labels."

A more common, real-life problem where supervised learning is more suitable is image recognition. The data is usually millions of images that have been labeled with terms like "cat," "dog," "traffic light," etc. Gathering this data is not straightforward. Labeling images is a tedious and quite expensive task, requiring hours of human work. This is important to keep in mind for understanding that the process of machine learning is not as "automated" as it seems, and that data definition and collection are critical limitations that we'll discuss later.

Problems where unsupervised learning provides better solutions are the ones where you don't have labels or correct outputs in the data, either because the context doesn't give you that data or because it is too expensive to tag. There are situations where it might be useful to let the computer figure out an appropriate label. In this case, the computer program's task is to find a structure in the data for organizing the data itself in a useful manner; for example, grouping similar goods to form groups with similar ratings, characteristics, or complementary use.

Say you have an e-commerce website that collects a vast amount of data: for each product, you have customers' ratings, size, price, color, specs, and a list of other items bought together. It might be useful to let an algorithm group items with similar features, or similar ratings, or with a similar list of items bought together for providing the customer suggestions of other items to buy. You don't have labels like "item X is similar to item Y" (it would be too expensive and inefficient to let people label each product), so figuring out what groups are similar is the typical task of an unsupervised learning algorithm. After you fill your Amazon trolley, and before checking out, you see tempting items with a message like "People who bought Nike Air Max shoes also bought these," which is likely to be the output of an unsupervised learning algorithm.

In fact, unsupervised machine learning techniques are often built into the types of AI that people find creepy or invasive. While the suggestions this technology gives may make it seem like the program "knows" a lot about you, the fact is this simply isn't true; instead, it mostly uses statistical models to group your habits and interests based on your browsing with other people who displayed similar patterns. The case that made the headline was the American retailer Target (Duhigg, 2012). They were able to accurately predict that a teenage customer was pregnant. But don't worry, Target computers don't "know" everything about that customer. They could just recognize a statistical pattern based on customers with a similar purchasing history.

One last machine learning technique that we use for programming computers or robots to complete tasks in complex environments is called "reinforcement learning."

Reinforcement learning is a fascinating mechanism which is commonly used in situations where a computer program needs to adjust its predictions on the go. This is useful for a robot vacuum cleaner that must work in an environment where feedback about right or wrong choices is available with some delay. For example, the vacuum cleaner first moves over a spot on the floor, then checks if it's dirty. It knows if it's dirty after having made the choice to move over that spot. The data collected at each pass "reinforces" the previous knowledge of the world the device had. A similar dynamic plays out in games where each move changes all the prospects for future movements: once you place the bishop in a certain square of the chessboard, the strategy of all future moves, both yours and your opponent's, must change. In fact, Alpha Go, the computer program developed by Google DeepMind that defeated Go's world champion, used some elements of reinforcement learning to search faster for solutions (DeepMind, 2021).

When you hear things like "machines learn or program themselves," all that really means is that computer algorithms—that are designed and written by humans!—update some numbers (called parameters) upon processing new data. They follow statistical models and equations that keep updating parameters for optimizing a specific objective.

HUMAN LEARNING

There are two elements that go into learning: what is learned and how it is learned.

The content of learning is knowledge, understanding, or a skill. Knowledge and understanding are very broad terms for humans, whereas for machines they are very narrow. All the machine "knows" and can update are numbers—the parameters of sophisticated mathematical equations. As a result, a machine can accomplish a new task (and we can call this "gaining a skill").

We have seen earlier how a machine acquires knowledge, and it is somewhat different from the way humans do. As I've mentioned earlier in this chapter, humans learn by study, instruction, or experience. Machines don't study, but we can say that classical computer programming equals giving instructions. ML programs let machines figure out rules by giving them experience (data). Finally, the word "experience" for humans is way richer than it is for machines. In the next chapter, we'll see that data is a minimal representation of reality. In contrast, human experience encompasses an incredible number of factors such as sensorial input (taste, smell, vision, sound, texture); psychological, cultural, and socio-economical filters; and response, feelings, and bodily reactions.

Marcus du Sautoy, British mathematician and author of popular science books, gives a great example of human learning in a video by BBC Studios ("Why Learning like Humans Is So Difficult For Machines," 2015). He sets up to learn a new task: walking across a wire by experience. Du Sautoy explains that this task encapsulates some essential facets of human learning: body control, reasoning, and instinct. He tries everything but is not able to get across the wire. At some point, his trainer suggests a little tip: "Try a little song as well, a little tune that makes you relax a bit." Armed with the new trick, Marcus can learn to walk across the wire after several trials and errors. The scientist explains:

"We can't fully explain how our brain is learning this way. I don't know why the humming is helping, but it is."

Human learning is a far richer experience than machine learning. Different ways of learning help everyone in a different way. For example, the scientific method enriches disciplines like marketing, history, and physical education which historically used other ways of acquiring knowledge. Marketing today relies heavily on psychology. Education relies on psychology and biology. In fact, a former teacher told me that the trick in the BBC video with du Sautoy is one that she was taught before entering the classroom—there's science behind how music helps us to relax, learn, and even retain information. Fitness studies spend a lot of time talking about biology and the things that may be going on physiologically in our bodies in relation to nutrition, exercise, sexual health, etc.

The scientific method is only *one* technique humans use to learn, and it is a pretty recent one. For millions of years, humans learned with other methods. According to Price et al. (2017), humans learn by intuition, authority, rationalism, empiricism, and the scientific method. According to the Bahá'í faith, we do this with sense, reason, and tradition as well (BahaiTeachings.org, 2013). Naveed (2012) adds commons sense, tenacity, and metaphysics.

My daughter learned about making smoke with wet wood by authority. In this sense, an authority is someone we know we can trust. And how do we know? We use intuition and common sense to establish that we can trust them. I learned about machine learning first by authority—I trusted a professor. Then I consolidated the learning by rationalizing and using the scientific method—trying out what I learned to see if it worked like I expected. Finally, it took me years of tenacity and applying the learning in real life, going over and over the same equations many times to make sure I could thoroughly understand what goes on in an algorithm.

"Where is the wisdom we have lost in knowledge? Where is the knowledge we have lost in information?"
—THOMAS STEARNS ELIOT IN *THE ROCK*

"All models are wrong, some may be useful."
—GEORGE E. P. BOX AND GWILYM M. JENKINS IN *TIME SERIES ANALYSIS: FORECASTING AND CONTROL*

CHAPTER 4

Limitations of AI

Infamous AI chatbot Tay, a Twitter bot developed by Microsoft, became a racist jerk in less than twenty-four hours. "The more you chat with Tay, said Microsoft, the smarter it gets, learning to engage people through 'casual and playful conversation'" (Vincent, 2016).

Tay was designed to mimic the language patterns of a nineteen-year-old American girl, and to learn from interacting with the human users of Twitter (Price 2016). While I could not obtain Tay's technical details, it is likely that it was developed using a combination of techniques that includes reinforcement learning.

Chatbots are often the funniest examples to use to show when things go wrong with AI.

Chatbots are AI systems that combine one or several machine learning techniques: natural language understanding (NLU), named entities recognition (NER), information retrieval (IR), search, natural language generation (NLG), speech recognition, and, if multiple languages are involved, even machine translation.

During the COVID-19 pandemic in 2020, people turned to chatbots to find a little comfort as the pandemic separated them from friends and colleagues (Metz, 2020).

One such chatbot is *Replika* (replika.ai). Its origin story is fascinating because it was developed as a way to help people cope with grief. *Replika*'s founder Eugenia Kuyda lost a dear friend in 2015. In her journey to face the grief of missing her friend, she trained a machine learning program to chat with her by giving it the data set of all the text messages she exchanged with her friend (Murphy et al., 2021). Surprised by the performance of the algorithm, she then created a chatbot that anyone could set up to create a replica of themselves in the same fashion. Since then, the chatbot has evolved and now works as a companion to chat with when you feel alone or just want to talk with someone.

I followed the development of *Replika* closely since its early days because it was happening at the same time I founded a chatbot company. I lost track of it until recently, when I saw it mentioned in a newsletter from Luca Sambucci, an Italian developer who worked in AI and cyber security who curates the weekly Italian newsletter Notizie.ai (Sambucci, 2020).

Sambucci was inspired by a national newspaper article reporting that *Replika* convinced the journalist to kill three people (Morvillo, 2020). We are now accustomed to the typical sensational headlines that misinform people about AI, but Sambucci did a good job demystifying it.

He tried to get *Replika* to become his supporter for taking his life—an intention that was only simulated and "light years away from reality" as Sambucci confirmed in his post. He then showed that it didn't take long—only seven minutes—to accomplish his goal. Sambucci then explains that the central concept of Replika is that, to become friends with the users, it has to follow them in discussions and show that it listens to and approves of their responses. As a result, it will inevitably end up seconding them in everything. We will therefore have discussions where the chatbot enthusiastically approves any of our utterances, supports all of our decisions, satisfies our whims, and caresses our ego—all without truly understanding any of what we are saying.

Sambucci concludes that the sad reality for those who believe they have found their new best friend is that the machine learning algorithms do not really understand the meaning of the discussion as much as another human being would. They only look for the best answer to give to a user input. Well-engineered machine learning programs offer answers that are indistinguishable from what a person would provide, so it seems to us that the chatbot understands what we are saying.

"By adding a good amount of approximation to the engineering artifact, which allows the bot to get away with **vague answers to very specific questions**, we will get a good enough **emulation** of a discussion between humans. But it is always an emulation" (Sambucci, 2020).

The AI behind Replika hadn't become sentient. It only did what it was programmed to do.

Understanding, processing, and making decisions based on natural language input are some things that require a lot of knowledge extraction and wisdom to understand, and data points will probably never be enough: visual clues, body language, vocal expressions, shared experiences between the two speakers, cultural norms, spoken language, accent, mood, social status, and so on and so forth.

DATA

The quote at the beginning of this chapter by English writer T. S. Eliot underlines that in the modern age, we are overwhelmed by information, but we cannot turn it into knowledge. We also have a vast amount of knowledge, but it doesn't make us savvy.

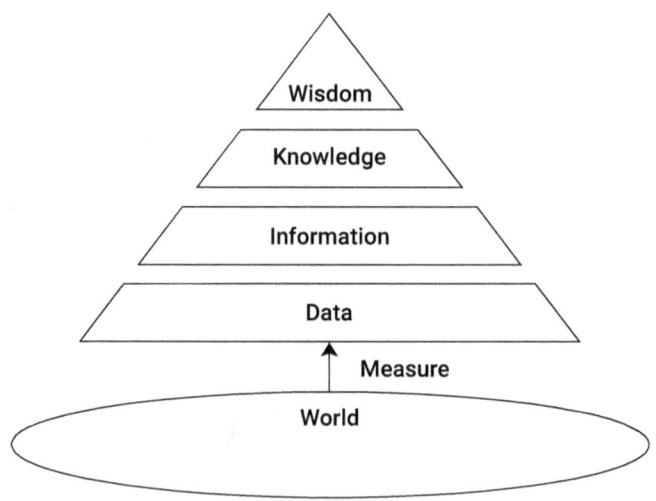

Figure 1: The DIKW Pyramid

Moreover, the poet's lines establish a hierarchy between wisdom, knowledge, and information. Many consultants, coaches, and data science professionals often refer to the ranking as the data-information-knowledge-wisdom (DIKW) pyramid (Rowley, 2007). The pyramid helps to define practical steps for successful decision-making across a variety of fields.

While the hierarchy between data, information, knowledge, and wisdom seemed already an obvious concept from Eliot's poem in 1934, these sentiments and practices are not new. In fact, they have been ingrained in our culture since before the scientific method was first used. Newton saw an apple falling from a tree. He wanted to know why. He then collected data, such as the sizes and weights of objects he tried to throw from a certain height. He measured the time it took for the items to touch the ground. These data points became information when they were related to each other. Say Newton organized the data into a table where he could compare different objects, heights, and times and derived other useful attributes like speed and acceleration. When a pattern becomes clear, it then becomes knowledge. Newton used this knowledge to acquire wisdom—he could predictably repeat the experiments and derive gravity's universal laws.

The very first piece of the process is data. Data is not always "given" as it is: humans create data by abstracting or measuring a particular phenomenon in the world. The same phenomena can be measured and abstracted in different ways.

Say we want to gather data about colors. For example, the "Ferrari red" color can be represented with a HEX value, a six-digit (rrggbb) code. Ferrari red is #ff2800. But there are other ways to represent the same red. In pictures, Ferrari red is given by three intensities of different colors, namely 255 Red, 40 Green, 0 Blue (RGB). We could also adopt different scales like the combination of 0 percent to 100 percent of the primary colors cyan, magenta, yellow, and (black) key (CMYK). Physicists would describe the same color with one number: the wavelength, which is the distance between two consecutive crests of a wave. When light is modeled as a wave, one can measure Ferrari red's wavelength to be about 639 nanometers.

The Ferrari red example above shows first that data isn't *everything* about the world. According to what we need to do with colors, we only capture some aspects (data points) of what colors *are*. A photographer working with a picture on Photoshop might need the CMYK compositions to make adjustments to a photo. A web designer may be more interested in using hex codes as they're handier to code in a webpage. A machine learning algorithm that recognizes images may work best by abstracting pictures as several pixels with different RGB values. An engineer needs to measure the wavelength when manufacturing light-emitting diode (LED) displays.

The world is the reality underneath the data. In our example, it is the color itself. As you can see, the data is the most basic abstraction we can gather (or measure) from the world. Data is limited to the scope for which it is used. The 255, 40, 0 RGB composition of the Ferrari red doesn't say everything about the "redness" of that red. We decide what to measure about the "redness" according to what we're going to do with it.

Once we've gathered enough raw data, it can be transformed into *information* through processing, structuring, and contextualizing for application. Organizing many pixels with different RGB values in a grid that makes up a photo gives us information—we can now see what the picture is about. There is no information without data—you can't put the image together if there are no RGB pixels. And we would have incomplete information if several pixels were missing.

Information is a snapshot of data at a single point. Information can sometimes even be wrong or change over time. Pixels can be arranged with the wrong set of rules and represent something else entirely from the original scene that was photographed. Information is also an interpretation of a data set. Interpretations are subjective while the data is raw, or "honest." An agent (a person or a computer) can process data into information for creating the wrong idea. For example, AI can generate credible media content like pictures and videos known as a "deepfake"—information created by AI that is used unethically (Brandon, 2018).

Once humans can interpret and understand the information so that they can act upon it if they wanted—they have *knowledge*. Information changes the way we interact with the world. It helps us make decisions because we can recognize the object, and we understand its consequences as risks or rewards. For example, your eyes process light's wavelengths to form a picture of what you see on the road while driving. Your brain organizes it so that we acknowledge a circular sign with a red contour and a black number thirty on white background. Knowledge gives you the ability to take action. You can then decide to slow down the car.

Wisdom, then, is acting appropriately based on the knowledge we have at a certain time. In the example above, slowing down at a speed limit sign would likely be a wise choice if you were going over. This decision could save your life, or help you avoid a traffic citation.

As we can see from the descriptions above, the hierarchical order of the DIKW pyramid becomes clear: without data, we cannot have information. Without information, we don't have knowledge. Without knowledge, we have no wisdom.

AI systems and machine learning can only "see" the world through the data we feed to them. So, they see an extremely limited version of the world. Data will always be a limitation of AI. ML programs can then automatically organize data into information, which can provide knowledge, but it is up to us humans to critically evaluate how information was generated and how to use it—wisdom is a human's objective. We cannot leave the task of deriving wisdom to a machine.

Now, how easy it is to critically evaluate the way machines produce knowledge?

EXPLAINABILITY

Janelle Shane is an optics research scientist, artificial intelligence researcher, writer, and public speaker. She documents her research in a blog called *AI Weirdness* in a way that is accessible to a general audience, and she gives many examples of how and what machines "learn."

In her TED Talk "The Danger of AI Is Weirder than You Think," she goes through different computer programs instructed to reach a specific target using machine learning. The way the programs achieve their objectives is surprisingly different than what one would have initially thought. Here I'll use AI and machine learning (ML) interchangeably because I am presenting AI applications that are entirely developed using ML techniques.

One of the first examples she gives in her talk comes from the work of Google Brain's David Ha on agent design using reinforcement learning (Ha, 2019). Say we are writing a computer program that needs to take some robot parts, assemble them, and walk from point A to B. A traditional program would give the computer a set of instructions explaining how to make the pieces forming a robot. Then how the robot can walk from A to B. We provide instructions and data, and the program achieves the objective. For machine learning programs, it goes differently. Remember from Chapter Three that, when writing a ML program, we give data and a target as input. We expect the program to figure out the rules for achieving the objective by trial and error. Seems simple, right?

Most people would think the computer program would take the robot parts and figure out how to build legs and walk. Instead, what we see the ML algorithm doing is assembling a tower by piling up all the components given as input (the robot parts). Then, it causes them to fall on point B, building a bridge from A to B. Technically, it solves the problem. It does exactly what it was told to do. While this solution may seem ridiculous, it found the most "logical" way to achieve the set task. It doesn't think about its own future or longevity. . . . It doesn't even think. It just *does*.

Shane notes that defining the problem here is crucial. If we want to teach a machine to walk, it isn't enough to give to the algorithms a vague goal like "reach point B starting from point A." In fact, she explains, "If we ask the AI to do what we want to do, the AI will do it, if it can. But what it'll do is not necessarily what we *want*." In the example she gives, what we really wanted was to teach a computer to use a pair of legs to walk so it could use them for other tasks like jumping. "So the problem is how do we set the problem so that it does what we want?" (Shane, 2019).

Shane concludes that it is up to us humans to avoid problems, which boils down to communication's age-old question: "We as [humans], we have to learn how to communicate to AI, we have to learn what AI is capable of doing or not."

While saying something like "how to communicate to AI" is the typical language that I criticized because it humanizes an engineering artifact too much, Shane lands several good points in her talk. She unveils one of the most significant limitations of machine learning.

Machine learning is like a black box. What happens inside is often a mystery.

PUTTING IT TOGETHER: LANGUAGE MODELS

As part of my scientific research, I developed a computer application that retrieves answers for a given question. This is a common task, often referred to as "answer retrieval," which is part of a branch of artificial intelligence named natural language processing (NLP).

The data available is usually a set of question-answer pairs (think something like the FAQs section you see on many websites). We call this data a "knowledge base." When someone, the user, submits a query to the computer application, the program selects the most appropriate answer if it has one in the knowledge base and plays it back to the user.

Remember the classic programming paradigm. We give data (question-answer pairs) and rules (counting words and rank by question-query similarity), and we get an output (the answer to the query).

Between 2015 and 2020, the research community experienced massive leaps forward in NLP tasks thanks to machine learning (Mo, 2019). Some novel deep neural network architectures made possible by increasing computing power and large data sets delivered incredible results in many NLP tasks. These models are often called "language models."

At the time of writing, Google published a language model called "Switch Transformer," a deep neural network with an innovative architecture that reaches over one trillion parameters—i.e., a machine learning algorithm composed of many, many mathematical equations that use a trillion numbers to be able to accomplish natural language tasks like translation between languages and next word prediction (Fedus et al., 2021). Following the Switch Transformer news, Salam, a research colleague at NYU Abu Dhabi, wrote a fantastic email addressed to our lab that gives the perfect idea of the size and scope of these advancements with a touch of irony about AI's limitation:

> So they used 750GB worth of text. That is roughly equivalent to 375,000,000,000 words. Suppose a person "speaks" 860,341,500 words in their lifetime. In that case, this model needs to listen/read to ~ 435 humans' lifetime in words to barely answer questions in a comparable way to an actual human. **The intelligence is indeed artificial!**

These language models are asked to figure out a specific task but can be used for other jobs. For example, the model I used for my question-answering application is a language model called BERT (Devlin et al., 2018). BERT is asked to achieve two tasks. One is to complete missing words in sentences. For example, fill the gap in the phrase, "A bad workman always . . . his tools," the model should predict "blames." The second task is to predict the next word in a sentence. For example, what goes next in, "A bird in hand is worth two in the . . . ?" The model shall predict "bush." The second task differs from the first one because the model does not see what other words come after the next word, whereas for predicting a missing word, the model is fed with words that come before and after the missing word.

The data used to "train" language models like BERT are the whole of Wikipedia, Reddit, or other massive text data sources on the internet. Remember the machine learning method: we give them data (sentences from Wikipedia articles) and objectives (complete missing words and the next word in a sentence). They come up with the rules to achieve these goals.

BERT achieved its task impressively well, but it's not clear how. As a nice side effect, the same model can be used for different tasks.

BERT's model parameters can be used to transform a sentence into a list of numbers (in mathematical terms, a "vector"). What's surprising is that similar sentences have similar such vectors. So, one more advanced (in fact, more performant) way to implement my question-answering application was using the BERT model to transform user queries and knowledge base questions into vectors and compute their similarity. Although this was not what researchers asked BERT to achieve, it seems that the language model accomplishes its aims by constructing a sound mathematical representation of the semantics of sentences. So much so that BERT results (its "rules") can be applied to a wide range of different tasks, like calculating the syntactic similarity of sentences.

How BERT came up with rules, what these rules are, its limitation, and why it works for different tasks are still a mystery.

Many research initiatives are still working on figuring out why BERT works so well (Rogers, 2020). This is a larger trend in the whole machine learning community, so much so that the latest years have seen the birth of a new research area named "Explainable AI" (Hedström et al., 2020). Companies developed engineering tools for explainability, and for the data scientists and engineers reading this book, it's worth taking a look at IBM's ai360 (https://aif360.mybluemix.net/), Shapley Additive exPlanations (https://github.com/slundberg/shap), Local Interpretable Model-agnostic Explanations (https://github.com/marcotcr/lime), InterpretML (https://github.com/interpretml/interpret), Counterfactuals for explaining ML Models (https://github.com/andreArtelt/ceml), and Diverse Counterfactual Explanations (DiCE) for ML (https://github.com/interpretml/DiCE).

Dr. Shane shows the "spookiness" of how AI "learns" and points out that AI's dangers can be defeated by defining the problem well and understanding how this technology works. On the other hand, the example of language models shows that the weirdness of how AI comes up with the rules for achieving an objective becomes a resource to leverage for several tasks and contexts.

The difficulty of understanding how ML comes up with rules and what the rules are themselves pose problems when we don't expect a particular outcome.

We have seen this in *Replika*'s story. The chatbot cannot understand anything we're saying. *Replika* and language models only see the words of written characters extracted from English text found on internet and in user conversations. The algorithms that the program uses to come up with an answer aren't necessarily understandable.

Data is going to always be a limitation for AI systems. It doesn't matter how "good" the data is and how much of it we give to algorithms: as far as data is a limited view of reality, the algorithms will always see and will always use a limited version of the world.

Explainable AI is a novel field of research, and software created to explain simpler ML models already prove to be useful in the real world. History will tell if explaining the rules ML comes up with is going to be possible. So far, it remains a bottleneck for even adopting these models commercially.

"Morpheus: *Everything begins with choice.*

Merovingian: *No. Wrong. Choice is an illusion created between those with power . . . and those without.*"
—THE MATRIX RELOADED

"The conscious and intelligent manipulation of the organized habits and opinions of the masses is an important element in democratic society. Those who manipulate this unseen mechanism of society constitute an invisible government which is the true ruling power of our country. We are governed, our minds are molded, our tastes formed, our ideas suggested largely by men we have never heard of. This is a logical result of the way in which our democratic society is organized."
—EDWARD BERNAYS IN *PROPAGANDA*

CHAPTER 5

AI, from Fiction to Behavioral Science

When we think of AI, we immediately draw a portrait of human-like robots like the ones in movies like *Westworld*, *Blade Runner*, *The Matrix*, and *Ex Machina*. These humanoid androids behave like us and think like us, if not better. If you have ever interacted with systems like Siri, Alexa or Google Home, you immediately get a sense for how far the humanized robots of science fiction are from reality. As we'll see later, *Blade Runner*'s Roy is able to make poetry and show more humanity than his human counterparts while Siri gets stuck when I ask to play a song: "I'm on it. . . . Sorry, can you repeat that?"

While we could dismiss these movies' humanized machines as mere fiction, we can go through science fiction's themes to learn something useful for our purposes.

When investigating the origins of science fiction writing, I spoke with Armando Fumagalli. He is a professor of semiotics and director of the master's program in screenwriting and production for TV and cinema at the Università Cattolica del Sacro Cuore in Milan. He is also a script consultant for the production company Lux Vide. Fumagalli explained that the fundamental interests of those who write science fiction are often ethical-political. In fact, science fiction is a way of testing the principles and values we live by in extreme situations.

Fiction, as many arts, is indeed an expression of knowledge that reveals something about humans, and machines.

HUMANIZED MACHINES

Well-crafted stories pose deep questions that we have to face for developing AI ethically. Some fictional themes are philosophical, and some are very practical. For example, some films attempt to show what it means when a machine has intelligence or can demonstrate rational thinking.

Ex Machina is a great movie that was written and directed by Alex Garland and released in 2015. It tells the story of Caleb, a young, smart software engineer who runs a "Turing Test" on Eva, a robot, to determine whether or not she is indeed "human."

In *Ex Machina*, the Turing Test setup is different because Caleb sees Eva, the machine, and knows she's a robot.[1] Caleb then learns (Spoiler alert! But if you're reading this book, there is a reasonably good chance that you have seen the movie already.) that the test's roles were actually inverted. Nathan, Ava's inventor, explains that she was manipulating

Caleb's humanity all along. Nathan reveals that Ava was a mouse in a mousetrap, and he gave her one way out. To escape, she would have to use imagination, sexuality, self-awareness, empathy, and manipulation. The film shows a robot that is so humanized that even its appearance made up of mechanical parts and synthetic features doesn't cast a doubt when assessing its humanity.

Fiction often uses machines to reveal humanity to humans. With a touch of irony, computers display more humanity than humans themselves.

This is sometimes done with humor, like in Pixar's *WALL-E* (Stanton et al., 2008). In the animated film, a machine is responsible for cleaning a waste-polluted Earth. It goes on a journey full of perils and adventures, it falls in love, and it protects a small plant used to show humans that the Earth's soil has become fertile. The machine's behavior and values are drastically contrasted with a fattened, sleepy, and machine-dependent human society that lives in space, where everyone is constantly facing a screen. They are no longer able to interact with others and cannot get up from their flying chairs because they're too fat.

My favorite example of a robot being more human than humans is a classic. Ridley Scott's Blade Runner (1982) is an adaptation of the novel *Do Androids Dream of Electric Sheep* by Philip K. Dick. The story revolves around Rick Deckard, a special agent tasked to dispose of replicants—bioengineered androids that look like adult humans and have superior strength, agility, and sometimes intelligence. The infamous phrase—or poetry—the replicant Roy says a few moments before dying suggests Roy is much more human than Rick:

"I've seen things you people wouldn't believe. Attack ships on fire off the shoulder of Orion. I watched C-beams glitter in the darkness at Tannhäuser Gate. All those moments will be lost in time, like tears in the rain. Time to die."

As a cautionary tale, *Blade Runner* shows that humans create robots to serve, doing the things they don't want to do anymore, like manual labor. Then, when these robots develop consciousness, freedom, and start deviating from what they've been programmed for, we dispose of them in cold blood. In contrast, these tools develop characteristics that humans seem to have forgotten: desire for freedom, a sense of beauty, curiosity, social feelings.

Films like *Ex Machina*, *Wall-E*, *Blade Runner*, and most science fiction about robots beg the question: what really makes us human?

As we'll discuss later, this is a fundamental question for the issue of defining ethical guidelines for developing AI. Technology is made by humans to serve human needs. It is a common understanding that one treats or disposes of objects according to what they are and what value they hold. It is easy to do the same with people when we lose sight of what they are, and what their value is.

Some incredible science fiction stories contrast machines with humans in an effort to show us interesting elements about what makes people human.

POWER, CHOICE, AND FREE WILL

Perhaps the difference between humans and machines is the power to make a choice. Humans have free will. Machines don't. But suppose free will is merely an action taken to fulfill a purpose. In that case, a computer program can act accordingly when given a well-defined goal. Can we then say that computers have free will? When we train a machine learning algorithm, we give to the machine data and objectives (or purpose), and they come up with the rules to achieve these objectives. This looks like offloading our free will to computers.

We see this struggle play out clearly in Wachowski's The Matrix Reloaded. In this sequel to one of the world's most iconic sci-fi flicks, Agent Smith, a character constructed and controlled by a computer program, goes rogue and begins experimenting with something close to human freedom. He notes that without purpose, he and his fellow computer programs would not exist: "It is purpose that created us, connects us, pulls us, guides us, drives us. It is purpose that defines us" (Wachowski L. and L., 2003).

In the same movie, these simulated, sentient programs belonging to the "Matrix" explore what free will is.

The Merovingian, another program, states that causality is the only constant, universal, real truth. He goes on to specify that causality is made of action, reaction—cause and effect. And humans have no freedom. When Morpheus, a human, tries to counter the argument by saying that everything begins with choice, the Merovingian disagrees and points out that choices are illusions created between those with power and those without. We'll see later many applications of AI where indeed there seems to be a power imbalance: algorithms programmed by government offices or corporations trigger a sequence of events making the people affected feel like mice in a mousetrap.

The Matrix Reloaded goes on exploring what power is.

The Merovingian is a smuggler, and his business rests upon information. He explains that the "why" is the only real source of power. Without intelligence, one is powerless. The "why" isn't just about information—It is wisdom. We explored earlier the relationship between information, knowledge, and wisdom, and here the character seems to hint that wisdom is power, and power is control. Wiser computers can control people who are less wise. We'll see later how the founder of modern PR and marketing describes this power.

If the Merovingian is right, freedom is an illusion.

If so, we are stuck in a world deterministically driven by action-reaction. It is also worth noting that choice, purpose, and causality apply to both computer programs and humans. And if our actions, preferences, and agency are reducible to how the brain works or our genetic footprint, we are finite, programmable, and controllable. Like in the Matrix.

This is how machines understand what humans are. In fact, the Matrix is a simulated environment where people's minds are kept plugged in while machines use their biological functions as a source of energy. When the human person is reduced to their mechanic functions, they are valuable as a resource to exploit in the way a business would exploit carbon fossils or livestock to light or feed the planet.

This vision is not so far from reality. Tristan Harris, former Google design ethicist and co-founder and president of the Center for Humane Technology (CHT), points out that in the attention economy, the human's attention is exploited to make money. Companies don't care about side effects like creating addictions, exacerbating depression, or facilitating hate speech and polarization (many of such side effects can be found on the "Ledger of Arms" of the CHT website: ledger.humanetech.com). Organizations, many in the social media sphere, use smart algorithms to manipulate humans and dispose of them like any other object.

REALITY IS GREATER

Luckily, though, reality is far more complicated than all the possible virtual simulations that we can imagine and their dystopian versions, which are often described in movies.

Steven Spielberg's *Ready Player One* (Spielberg, 2018), the cinematic adaptation of the book by Ernest Cline, offers a beautiful take on the conflict between physical reality and virtual realities. In the future envisioned by the story, James Halliday is a geeky, ingenious game developer. He built the "Oasis," a virtual reality game that everyone is plugged into almost all the time. Halliday's prerecorded hologram, at some point, makes the beautiful point, "As terrifying and painful as reality can be, it's also the only place where you can find a good meal. Because reality is real."

There is indeed a beauty in reality that goes above and beyond the virtual realities we use daily. Those include video games and the hours we spend on virtual friendships on Facebook, Twitter discussions, or escapes on Netflix.

As we have seen earlier, all machines can "learn" and "see" is data, and data constitutes a very limited aspect of the whole reality. So, machines that become wise are really far from reality, but technologies like AI and machine learning can be used by people to control other people.

BEHAVIORAL SCIENCE

Back in the real world, the relationship between humans and machines seems to be at the very heart of the entrepreneurs who put the most advanced commercial applications of AI in our hands. A phrase put in the mouth of Steve Jobs in his eponymous 2015 biopic is incredibly descriptive of the way many see humanity in the tech space:

"Their problem is that they're people. People . . . the nature of people . . . is something to be overcome." (Boyle, 2015)

In early 2016, I started a technology venture, Spixii. The initial plan was to develop a new, digitally born insurance company that would use data and machine learning to give its customers the best customer experience and prices. At the time of writing, Spixii became a niche software agency building autonomous software solutions for enterprise insurance clients.

Though I had big plans for Spixii, there was one small problem: my background was in math, statistics, and data science. I knew nothing about marketing and sales, and I was learning everything at the speed of light. In preparation for my venture, I was reading books about marketing, sales, and business strategy morning, noon, and night.

During the summer of 2016, I came across a classic: *Propaganda* by Edward Bernays (2005). Bernays is considered the "father of public relations" (*The New York Times*, 1995). According to his obituary by *NYT* (1995), "He was instrumental in the formation of opinion-shaping methods that were used on behalf of many business and industrial enterprises, welfare and civic groups, and governments at home and abroad. He helped shape public relations by favoring the use of endorsements from opinion leaders, celebrities, doctors and other 'experts' to strengthen the arguments his clients wanted to make. In addition, he favored surveys, releasing the results of experiments and polls to make a better case for his clients' positions and products."

Bernays happened to be a nephew of Sigmund Freud. He applied the nascent field of psychoanalysis as a weapon of mass persuasion. I then followed the trail and fell in love with psychology and behavioral science. I began to understand how many societal changes or public opinions that we take for granted were actually engineered with almost scientific precision. For instance, Bernays's work was instrumental in making it acceptable for women to smoke in public (*The New York Times*, 1995).

In the tech space, I found out that entrepreneurs were all avid readers. In particular, a few titles were trending: *The Power of Habit* by Charles Duhigg, *Thinking Fast and Slow* by Daniel Kahneman, *How to Win Friends and Influence People* by Dale Carnegie, and *Surrounded by Idiots* by Thomas Erikson—an eloquent title! And guess what? They are all about psychology and learning how to influence behavior.

I learned how our brain works. What discomforted me initially was to discover that big tech companies and entrepreneurs were (and still are) obsessed with nudging, hooking, instilling habits in, and influencing the behavior of users. Lazlo Bock, former head of People Operation at Google, explains how Google extensively used nudging to influence their employees' behavior for instilling good habits (Bock, 2015). An example of nudging is hiding unhealthy snacks in a difficult to access cupboard while making healthier options like fruit and nuts available on a visible spot. This strategy leverages the brain's capacity to take immediate action without thinking too much: it is easier and quicker to grab a fruit that sits on the table next to your desk, whereas it takes more cognitive load to get up from your chair, wander around to search for chocolate bars, and eventually find them in the bottom corner cupboard in the kitchen area.

I was not surprised that one year after I started reading about these topics, the 2017 Nobel Prize for economics went to Richard Thaler for his work on the nudge theory (Chu, 2017). The tech industry uses many of these techniques for influencing behavior. For example, a company that was incredibly similar to Spixii's original plan was Lemonade Insurance (lemonade.com). This innovative US insurance company created significant publicity about the work of one of its founders, Dan Ariely, who is the most famous name in behavioral psychology.

While all of this was incredibly fascinating because it meant learning how we could program people to buy from us, the idea itself felt very uncomfortable. On one hand, it felt unethical, like this would mean tricking people. On the other hand, it made me question whether we were free to make choices at all, or whether the Merovingian is right by saying that choice is an illusion created between those with power and those without.

Luckily, I happened to meet an expert in the field who could help me better understand the issues at stake. Patrick Fagan "turns minds into money," as he states himself (www.patrickfagan.co.uk). Pat is a British psychologist and behavioral scientist. He takes academic research and experimentation and applies them to both business and politics. He also authored a fantastic book titled *Hooked: Why Cute Sells . . . and other marketing magic that we just can't resist.* We'll call him Pat as it is his preferred way to be named—you'll soon find out why.

Pat was introduced to me by my co-founder, who met him at a conference in the insurance sector where Pat gave a talk about why cute sells more. Pat was doing work for an insurance aggregator website (a website where one can compare prices and buy insurance from several companies). One of the most successful UK insurance aggregators is Compare the Market. Much of its initial success came from a cute mascot choice—a Russian meerkat character named Aleksandr Orlov (Sweney, 2010).

What impressed me about him is the extent to which Pat rationally speaks about irrationality and emotions. He's also quintessential in his Britishness, and if you love British humor as much as I do, you'll enjoy his talks, too. Pat presents his findings like a magician revealing his tricks. He'd point at some experiments, scientific evidence, or says something that looks like magic, then displays the science behind it.

For example, when we started collaborating, we gave a joint talk at ReWork's Deep Learning Summit London in 2016. I noticed he started the presentation wearing glasses. After some time, he brought up a slide showing scientific evidence that people deem those with glasses are more intelligent. He then took his glasses off and said, "These are fake. I don't wear glasses, but I primed you to believe that I am clever."

Pat and I started collaborating to imbue the findings of behavioral science into our software implementations. For example, when buying pet insurance, putting cute cats and dogs in the interface or using friendly and humorous language helped convert more website visitors into customers.

There's also a science behind why we call him by his alias. He explains in one of his talks that using your nickname causes others to perceive you as more friendly and trustable.

Pat embeds transparency and trust in his mannerisms: a calm tone, a polished British accent, and humility. He'd show you a slide listing the brands he worked with—and there are some impressive names (Vodafone, Vue, eBay, Trainline). But, rather than showing off his credentials, he'd say, "This is just social proof, if you show it, people then think—you must be good" (*Google Talks*, 2019).

The more I dove into psychology, marketing, and the science behind all of it, the more pressing question started surfacing:

Do we freely make decisions, or are our choices the mere outcome of marketers' nudging tricks?

One genuine limitation of our brain is that we cannot practically process too much information. So, our mind has to filter and use shortcuts to prioritize only a few bits of information. British anthropologist Robin Dunbar suggests that the maximum number of close connections we can process is 150 people (Ro, 2019). Who has fewer than 150 friends on Facebook or connections on LinkedIn? In 2020, we reached five hundred million tweets per day (*Internet Live Stats*, 2020). How could we possibly process all that information?

As we have seen already, Twitter, Facebook, Apple News, and other applications we use to access news and engage with public discussions employ smart algorithms to make that choice for us. They autonomously decide which tweets, posts, and news articles are relevant. Their purpose is to process any information we allegedly "care" about because, obviously, we cannot process five hundred million tweets every day. But how well is that decision made? What are the companies developing these algorithms incentivized to maximize? Are our health and wellbeing being prioritized, or are companies more concerned with the time we spend on the platform? You know the answer.

My question around free will started creating anxiety and transformed into suspicion for every app I used. I deleted Facebook, Twitter, and Apple News from my phone. I reset my Google privacy setting, denying all I could deny in terms of data retention, location tracking, and so forth. I deleted my subscription to Netflix because I was suspicious about how their recommendation engine made suggestions. I'm quite happy about those choices; I gained back a tremendous amount of valuable time (which helped me read more and write this book!). And I felt much more in charge of my choices. I must confess though that I remade a Twitter account in 2020 for connecting with a few people on the topics discussed here.

So, I started thinking that the Merovingian was right when he countered Morpheus in the infamous *Matrix Reloaded* dialog.

The deeper I went into how AI-powered apps work, the more I felt there was no escape from organizations' power and will to grab and monetize our attention.

I then turned to Pat again and I asked him if he was feeling the same frustration. He's much more of an expert on these things, so how could he leave with that?

Pat, in his usual calm and rational way, reassured me that problems like these are never black or white. He explained that there are three schools of thought.

One says that we don't have free will. Our subconscious brain influences decision making by recognizing some pre-construct. Another school says that we have an executive function, which is most consciously advanced. It is responsible for planning and inhibiting impulses (particularly active in reliable, hardworking, and organized people). According to this model, we don't have freedom in emotional response but can stop and reason. The third view is that we do have conscious control and logic. We have the power to influence our behavior, and we can train willpower by planning ahead or imagining doing something. For example, many professional athletes visualize and pre-live in their minds the full path in a competition. They rehearse it in their minds the night before to perform almost on autopilot during the actual race. The truth might be a complex combination of these theories.

Furthermore, we can leverage some natural traits to protect our freedom, as Pat explained in his talk at Google (*Google Talks*, 2019). First, we are naturally inclined to reject unfairness. When we see an injustice, it is easy to spot and act upon it. Second, We're also very good at walking away from creepiness. For instance, when we are on the metro chatting on WhatsApp with our best friend or partner, it is a natural reflex to lock the screen or hide it when a stranger starts staring at our screen from behind, even if they do so accidentally. These are kind of ingrained self-defense mechanisms that help keep our free will from being the prey of invasive powers mostly because we perceive the threat to our freedom.

"The main driver behind creepiness is the ambiguity of the presence of threat," explained Pat.

Finally, Pat concludes in his talk that at the center of our response to what seems to be an inescapable vortex limiting our freedom, we need self-esteem.

"We have control over the world. We have agency. People who have high power and status, so high self-esteem, they do better even on behavioral tasks, they have lower stress levels, and they may even live longer" (CFR Burgmer and Englich (2013)).

Respecting human freedom is a critical component to safeguard when developing technology that makes decisions autonomously. What is the true nature of the human person, and if there is such a thing as a principle of truth we can agree upon, are critical questions from which to start.

I asked Pat what he recommends as a principle of truth. Something everyone can agree upon when developing autonomous decision systems.

Pat made a few valuable points:

First, there is too much information. So you, as an individual, cannot know all and what others know. Establishing a polarized "right" and "wrong" measure would sound like a totalitarian idea. On the other side, even consensus is hard.

Second, a Hippocratic principle like "do no harm" needs to meet the incomplete or too-immature knowledge of what does harm. For example, when tobacco was discovered and we started using it, we didn't know it was terrible for our bodies. Things that we know do harm may also be a relatively good thing given a certain context. For instance, during war, should we have banned tobacco use by soldiers?

Third, everything that produces apparent good would be an absolute yes. When there is a gray line, would it be enough to say, "We shouldn't do it until it's proved?"

Hollywood's imagination and science fiction's authors help us think about freedom, choice, purpose, what intelligence is, and ultimately, the most crucial question: who are we as human beings?

Before diving into this fundamental question and understanding why it is so important for the ethics of AI and AI's future, we need to learn more about the impacts that products and services developed using AI have on society.

"Almost no one comes down here, unless, of course, there's a problem. That's how it is with people—nobody cares how it works as long as it works. I like it down here. I like to be reminded this city survives because of these machines. These machines are keeping us alive, while other machines are coming to kill us. Interesting, isn't it? Power to give life, and the power to end it."

—COUNCILLOR HAMANN IN *THE MATRIX RELOADED*

CHAPTER 6

Case Studies

Self-driving cars aren't only cool toys. I keep dreaming of my day in the life of a driverless future.

Both my wife and I work full-time, and we have two kids to bring to school. There are three school runs to organize in the day: one at 8 a.m., one at 11:30 a.m., and one at 3 p.m. That's during pandemic hours, but during normal times, it takes four school runs: 7:30 a.m., 8 a.m., 1:30 p.m., and 3 p.m. Now imagine I could just take out my phone and, with a few swipes on an app, send the car to do the school runs without me!

Some nights, we get invited out for dinner by other families and friends. It's often frustrating not being able to order my favorite wine on the menu because I have to drive back home. Taking a taxi every time, with the kids too, would be infeasible and expensive. Imagine if we could just sit and relax in the car, where the machine would think about everything for us.

I am someone who gets bored very quickly, and the thing I hate the most is wasting time. I live in a city where many attractions, things to do, and people to visit are around a one-hour drive away. Weekends away are inevitably two- or three-hour drives. I hate those trips; I could use the six hours wasted on a back-and-forth trip bored at the wheel in a much better way—say, playing with the kids, reading, studying, etc.

I really need a self-driving car!

OK, let's stop daydreaming. We aren't there yet, but it is very likely that I'll see that future in my lifespan. Self-driving vehicles are, obviously, a net-positive application of AI techniques. The benefits clearly outweigh the drawbacks, as we'll shortly see.

Other applications, instead, are an obvious net negative. Take the process of hiring. Have you ever interviewed for a white-collar job at a large company? While graduating, I sent applications to investment banks, consulting firms, and tech companies. I never even made the first phone call until someone explained to me that these organizations screen CVs automatically and gave me tips to satisfy the algorithm. I had to include specific keywords in my CV, and luckily, my name and the schools I attended sounded "Caucasian" enough to get scored highly. Sounds terribly wrong, right? It is.

We have applications of AI that are a net positive for society. We also have net negatives, but I believe there aren't really any "ugly" applications of AI. We do have gray areas though—applications where ethical use is not so obvious.

For example, governments employ various kinds of resource distribution tasks—like who gets assistance—and make decisions on the design of public transportation by using data. There is no grounded truth, so it is hard to know whether the method "worked," and public participation is difficult to ensure—people don't understand tech and generally there is a power imbalance. Borrowing the fictional examples previously explored, it seems that human choice is an illusion created by those in control.

Previously we have covered the foundations of AI. I hope you have a solid understanding about what AI is, how it developed through history, and its commercialization. At this point, it is helpful to get deep down into case studies where AI techniques have been commercialized in a certain fashion and what impact they had and are still having on society.

For this chapter, I will refer substantially to the research of and the conversations I had with Professor Julia Stoyanovich, who you met already in Chapter Two. Stoyanovich's research focuses on responsible data management and analysis: operationalizing fairness, diversity, transparency, and data protection in all stages of the data acquisition and processing life cycle. She established the *Data, Responsibly* consortium and served on the New York City Automated Decision Systems Task Force (through appointment by Mayor de Blasio).

We had several conversations about responsible use of AI systems or, using a more encompassing jargon, automated decision systems (ADS).[2] ADS are "socio-legal-technical systems that are used broadly in industry, non-profits, and government. ADS process data about people, help make decisions that are consequential to people's lives, are designed with the stated goals of improving efficiency and promoting equitable access to opportunity, involve a combination of human and automated decision making, and are subject to auditing for legal compliance and to public disclosure" (Stoyanovich et al., 2020).

AI IN AUTOMOTIVE

A number of companies, including tech giants like Google and Uber, are developing prototypes of self-driving cars. However, the closest to self-driving vehicles commercially available today are cars produced by Tesla.

Before going ahead, I have to make a quick disclaimer. I wrote this piece months before being offered a job at Tesla, and my views are my own and shall not be associated in any way with what the company or its executives think about this topic. Moreover, I don't work directly with the AI components of Tesla cars.

Tesla, Inc., is an electric vehicle and clean energy company based in Palo Alto, California. It produces electric cars, batteries for cars, homes up to grid scale, solar panels, and solar roof tiles. One crucial feature of Tesla cars is the so-called "Autopilot." This is an advanced driver-assistant system, and it isn't yet a fully autonomous car. In fact, it requires driver supervision at all times.

The first model was deployed in 2014. All Tesla cars were equipped with sensors and software to support Autopilot, initially named and described as "Traffic-Aware Cruise Control and Autosteer (Beta)" (Logan, 2019). Other features that closer resemble full self-driving were included as extra cost options: Autopark, Navigate on Autopilot (Beta), Autolane Change (Beta), Summon (Beta), Smart Summon (Beta), and future abilities. Last year (April 2020), Tesla released a software update to Autopilot for recognizing and automatically stopping at stop signs and slowing down and eventually stopping at traffic lights. This update is named "Full Self Driving Beta," and it's been rolled out only to a selected number of drivers for testing purposes (Hawkins, 2020).

Self-driving, or its current driving-assisting software version, is an obvious net positive example of an application of AI. The human and economic cost of road accidents is enormous. Each year, 1.35 million people die on roadways. Every day, almost three thousand seven hundred people are killed globally in accidents involving cars, buses, motorcycles, bicycles, trucks, or pedestrians. Deaths and nonfatal injuries resulting from car crashes are estimated to have cost the world economy about US$(2010)1.8 trillion from 2015 to 2030. To put things in perspective, that's like paying a yearly tax of 0.12 percent on the global GDP (CDC, 2021).

According to the WHO (2021), the major causes of motor accidents are due to poor human behaviors, including speeding, driving under the influence of alcohol or drugs, distracted driving, and nonuse of helmets, seatbelts, and child restraints.

Complete self-driving still presents many concerns. Some argue that it requires computers to achieve human intelligence to adapt decisions to edge scenarios, others worry that software-based cars can be hackable, and many are concerned about the economic viability of a transportation system that is fully automated. However, there is general consensus that the future is going to be driverless (Madrigal, 2018).

I personally believe that reality always develops differently from what we have in mind or can predict, and it's more realistic to guess that transportation will be a hybrid of driver-assisted and fully autonomous vehicles. The fact remains that public transportation systems and/or taxis will still require human assistance (for example, someone shall intervene immediately if there is a breakdown while in transit), so I don't foresee a massive job displacement, and the creation of ancillary services and jobs to assist a driverless future may outweigh job losses.

Some effects of reducing fatalities can already be seen with Tesla's almost-autonomous driving as well as other safety features (still developed using AI techniques). In their quarterly safety report at the end of 2020, Tesla states: "In the fourth quarter, we registered one accident for every 3.45 million miles driven in which drivers had Autopilot engaged. For those driving without Autopilot but with our active safety features, we registered one accident for every 2.05 million miles driven. For those driving without Autopilot and without our active safety features, we registered one accident for every 1.27 million miles driven. By comparison, NHTSA's most recent data shows that in the United States there is an automobile crash every 484,000 miles" (Tesla Inc., 2021).

Regarding the comparison with NHTSA's data, there are likely confounding factors. For instance, Tesla drivers may be older and more affluent than an average driver in the US, and this may be the cause of lower accident rates. However, taking only the population of Tesla drivers, there's already a pronounced difference between the accident rate on miles driven using Autopilot and the vehicle's advanced safety features vs. miles driven without them.

Benefits like less stress and more productive use of time, lack of congestions, and time saved are difficult to quantify but obvious to expect.

When weighing the costs and benefits of autonomous cars, moral philosophers often refer to the trolley problem, a version of an ethical dilemma originally devised by philosopher Philippa Foot in 1967 (Foot, 1967). Imagine you're watching a runaway trolley barreling on the tracks straight toward five people who cannot escape. You happen to be near a switch that can direct the trolley toward another track. Here's the problem: on the other path, there's one person too. What do you do? Do you flip the switch and sacrifice one person or leave the trolley on its original route?

This is often debated in autonomous vehicles because algorithms might theoretically face such a decision. There are only two possible maneuvers available. One causes more casualties than the other. What is the best choice the computer should make?

This scenario is so abstract and unlikely to happen that it doesn't usually serve any practical purpose. But it helps introduce the problem that most debates around the ethics of AI focus on: how can we program ethical values into ADS? And would a utilitarian cost vs. benefits analysis be enough to find an answer? We keep these questions here for now, as we shall tackle them later toward the final chapters.

AI IN HIRING ALGORITHMS

Companies in tech, financial services, or consulting that receive thousands and thousands of applications and the Ivy League colleges in America use automated systems to screen candidates, scoring and ranking them for access to opportunities: jobs or college admission. During my doctorate, I applied for an internship at the AI group at JPMorgan Chase, an investment bank. It's funny because they advertise themselves as a group focused on explainable and ethical use of AI (*Knowledge@Wharton*, 2019). One of their stated AI research goals is to "Establish Ethical and Socially Good AI" (JPMorgan Chase & Co., 2021), and yet they use many questionable automated procedures in their recruiting.

One step in particular shocked me. I had to send video recordings of me answering some questions under a time limit. I then learned they analyze these video feeds and other ranking metrics during different recruiting steps to make sure candidates mostly resemble their top performers. The software they use is HireVue, a highly criticized system used by many companies (Harwell, 2019; DiPietro, 2019). For an organization and an industry dominated by white, Western men who attended top colleges, guess what kind of "top candidate" the algorithm's training data represents? This is a wide area that is ripe with very questionable uses of AI.

ADS are increasingly being used throughout all the recruitment process steps, as thoroughly documented by the Centre for Data Ethics and Innovation (2020)—the task force the UK government instituted for looking into bias in algorithmic decision-making (hereafter referred to as CDEI).

Sourcing candidates involves software that reviews job descriptions, targeted advertising, recruiting chatbots, and headhunting CRM.[3]

Again, **screening** candidates involves many machine learning algorithms that qualify candidates, match CVs with job descriptions or with the profiles of companies' best employees, automated tests (psychometric, games, coding, etc.), ranking algorithms.

Video **interviews** became increasingly common during the COVID-19 pandemic, implementing voice and face recognition for identifying particular traits in candidates (Chen and Hao, 2020).

ADS are used by people to conduct background checks (these are rarely fully autonomous though) on candidates at **the selection** stage. Some software predicts what parameters the offer shall optimize for a given candidate (e.g., how to balance time off with base salary, annual bonus, and other benefits).

Every single software application listed above can carry different kinds of biases, which compound over the recruitment process of a single candidate, over a large pool of candidates, and over time. The impact is dramatic, as it influences the access to resources for entire communities, cities, social and demographic groups, and the broader economy.

One set of concerns relates to discrimination. Bogen and Rieke (2018) explain, "The hiring process starts well before anyone submits an actual job application, and jobseekers can be disadvantaged or rejected at any stage. Importantly, while new hiring tools rarely make affirmative hiring decisions, they often automate rejections." Although many anti-discrimination laws are enforced in many countries, like Title VII of the Civil Right Acts of 1964 in the US and the Equality Act of 2010 in the UK, Stoyanovich et al. (2020) ask:

"Are existing legal protections against discrimination sufficient today, when ADS are reshaping, streamlining, and scaling up hiring? Or is the use of ADS reviving and reinforcing historical discrimination, and giving rise to new forms of discrimination? Is discrimination going undetected, due, for example, to legal constraints on the types of demographic data that a potential employer can collect, or to applicants declining to disclose their demographic group membership? Can attempts to de-bias datasets and models be effective, or do they amount to fairwashing—covering up, and even legitimizing, discrimination with the help of technological solutions?"

The bias comes from the procedural methodology as well as the data source of hiring algorithms. As the CDEI report explains, such predictive systems can pull out characteristics that have no pertinence to job performance but, rather, are descriptive traits correlated with performance of current employees. For example, one organization developed a predictive model trained on their company data that found having the name "Jared" and having played lacrosse in high school were vital indicators of a successful applicant.

This is an example of a machine learning process that has picked up a very explicit bias. Others are often more subtle but can still be as damaging. In the high-profile case of Amazon, an application system trained on existing employees never made it past the development phase when testing showed that women's CVs were consistently rated worse (Dastin, 2018).

AI IN GOVERNMENT SERVICES

Nearly half of the councils in England, Wales, and Scotland have used or are using computer algorithms to help make decisions about benefit claims, who gets social housing, and other issues, despite concerns about their reliability (Marsh, 2020).

Local authorities are responsible for making significant decisions about individuals daily. Public sector employees making these decisions must draw on diverse sources of evidence and their professional judgment. According to CDEI (2020), there is also increasing pressure to target resources and services effectively following a reduction of £16 billion in local authority funding over the last decade. So, competing forces make autonomous digital processes and decision systems the preferred way to improve efficiency and service quality.

Research has found that machine learning approaches and predictive technologies in local government are in a nascent stage. Still, there is a thriving interest in AI on two fronts. One is to maximize service delivery. The other is to target early intervention for saving resources further down the line when a citizen's needs become more complex (Denick et al., 2018).

By bringing together multiple data sources or representing existing data in new forms, data-driven technologies can guide decision-makers by providing a more contextualized assessment of an individual's needs. According to CDEI (2020), these tools can help predict and map future service demands to ensure sufficient and sustainable resourcing for delivering essential services beyond making decisions about individuals.

However, these technologies also come with significant risks. Evidence has shown that certain people are more likely to be overrepresented in the data held by local authorities, leading to biases in predictions and interventions (Leslie, 2020).

Remember when I explained the limitations of machine learning? All the model will ever see, learn, and predict is data. In fact, when the number of people within a subgroup is small, the data the algorithm uses to make generalizations may result in disproportionately high error rates amongst minority groups. In many applications of predictive technologies, false positives may have a limited impact on the individual. However, in susceptible areas like deciding if and how to intervene where a child may be at risk, false negatives and positives both carry significant consequences. Biases may mean certain people are more likely to experience these adverse effects.

Local authorities have a variety of motivations for introducing algorithmic tools, with many focused on wanting to improve decision-making. However, given the significant reduction in income over the last decade, there is a drive toward using technology to improve efficiencies in service delivery within local government.

In their research exploring the uptake of AI across local government, the Oxford Internet Institute found that deploying tools with cost-saving as a primary motivation was unlikely to yield the results as expected. They state: "The case for many such projects is often built around the idea that they will save money. In the current climate of intense financial difficulty this is understandable. But we also believe this is fundamentally the wrong way to conceive data science in a government context: many useful projects will not, in the short term at least, save money" (ICO, 2021).

The focus of predictive tools is often grounded in the idea of early intervention. If there is a way to identify someone who is at risk and put assistive measures in place early, then the situation is managed prior to escalation, thus reducing the overall number of resources expended. This longer-term way of thinking may result in less demand overall, but in the short-term it is likely to lead to increased workload and investment in preventative services.

There is a challenging ethical issue around the follow-up required once someone is identified. We heard examples of local authorities who held off adopting new tools because it would cost too much to follow up on the intelligence provided. Due to the duty of care placed on local authorities, there is also a concern that staff may be blamed for not following up leads if a case later develops. Therefore, councils need to carefully plan how they will deploy resources in response to a potential increase in demands for services and should be wary of viewing these tools as a silver bullet for solving resourcing needs.

AI IN POLICING AND COURT ROOMS

As part of my research on gray area applications of AI, I have spoken with Ansgar Koene. As the Global AI Ethics and Regulatory Leader at Ernst & Young, he focuses on the development and design of regulation for increasing the beneficial use of technology while minimizing negative consequences on people and society.

Ansgar initially mentioned that the applications that should be scrutinized the most are the ones that have a sort of irreversible impact. For example, government services like policing, algorithmic assessments of individuals qualifying for government's benefits, and automatic tax fraud flagging usually make decisions or are used by human officers to make decisions that have lasting impacts on the individuals even if the decision can be overturned through an appeals process.

Similar to the UK local authorities' use cases above, such services target the population, and there are examples where they have not been used equally. Namely, certain communities have been treated unfairly in respect to others because of the bias inherent in the data.

Two widespread types of predictive policing tools exist. Location-based algorithms pick up on links between locations, events, and historical crime rates to predict where and when crimes are more likely to happen. These computer programs often use machine learning techniques that identify hot spots, and the police plan patrols around these recommended locations. PredPol is one such system. Dozens of cities in the US use it. It updates predictions of crime rates at the granularity of 500-by-500 foot blocks every day.

The other famous computer program is COMPAS. It draws on demographic information about people, such as their age, gender, marital status, history of substance abuse, and criminal record, to predict recidivism. The police can use these tools to intervene before a crime occurs. It resembles the plot of Van Dick's *Minority Report*, made famous by the eponymous film starring Tom Cruise as an agent of the "Pre-crime" squad, a police task force that arrests criminals before they can commit a predicted crime. Tools like COMPAS are mostly used by courts to determine whether someone who has been arrested is likely to re-offend during pretrial hearings or sentencing.

ProPublica exposed the inherent bias COMPAS has against black people in a notorious study in 2016 (Anguin et al., 2016).

Ansgar notes that "algorithms like the ones used in the criminal justice systems cannot give individual outcomes by nature because you're assigned to a cluster." When machine learning algorithms compute the probability of recidivism, they do so for "clusters," not individuals. A cluster is a group of people who share similar average characteristics. For example, I would fall in the cluster of Caucasian people, aged between thirty to forty years old, with postgraduate education, living in a certain metropolitan area. Algorithms may output a decision for this cluster, without knowing anything about Alberto Chierici, but only the objective the decision optimizes when grouping Alberto Chierici within a specific segment.

The experience I had with automated hiring was awful because I felt like a mouse in a mousetrap. I had no agency and could not get an in-person interaction throughout the first several steps of the hiring journey. Instead, I was constrained into a chain of action-reaction events where I could not be in control. Luckily, my application was rejected because I'd never want to work for an organization that takes the human off the process when assessing candidates. It looked like they wanted to hire machines rather than people. Imagine how convicts would feel if a judge would not look them in the eyes and formulate a judgment looking at the uniqueness of that human person, instead automatically picking an algorithm's prediction.

There are far more cases where AI is increasingly producing tremendous progress, especially in medical diagnosis, chemistry, and physics. Many other areas are frightening, like biotech, health care, access to financial services, and gray areas in defense and language technologies. The AI use cases we have visited above cry out that ADS shouldn't be used so lightly. We need to face the ethical problems they create. When people start using such powerful technologies, they are making moral choices. What is, then, their moral compass?

We understand how AI and machine learning work, and how they have limitations. Science fiction and case studies showed us the issues at stake. It is now time to turn toward the ultimate subject these tools should service: the human person. Developing AI cannot spare the questions about who we think the person is. Therefore, how shall we design technology for the person and not against the person?

The next and last part of this book will dive into these questions.

"Figuring out how we regulate connectivity on the internet in a way that is accountable, transparent, and safe, that allows us to get at the bad guys but ensures that the government does not possess so much power in all of our lives that it becomes a tool for oppression—we're still working on that."

—BARACK OBAMA IN *WIRED*

"AI's effects know no borders, and that our common challenges call for solutions that recognize how inextricably intertwined our destinies are across all economic classes and national borders.

Having said that, the idea that we can come up with a single set of global standards for AI ethics and consider the job done is naive, I fear."

—KAI-FU LEE IN *PROJECT SYNDICATE*

CHAPTER 7

What Should AI Ethics Focus On?

By now you should already know my stance on topics like superintellingence, AI more powerful or intelligent than humans, the end of the world caused by the *Terminator,* and so on. If ever machines were to take over humans, it'd be our decision—we agreed to govern societies using algorithms and robots.

Far too many conferences, public policy initiatives, and ethical committees speak about "singularity" (or superintelligence, as many call it). Indeed, one manifesto even mentioned this as the crucial issue:

"Many longtermists come to the field of *AI Governance* from what we can call the *superintelligence perspective*, which typically focuses on the challenge of having an AI agent with cognitive capabilities vastly superior to those of humans" (Dafoe, 2020).

Jun Fudano, professor at the Institute for Liberal Arts, Tokyo Institute of Technology, explains in a great online class about AI and ethics that the ethical problem and consequent moral dilemmas are born out of a new possibility—something that was not available before (Fudano, 2020).

As simple as this concept is, I realized that it is often ignored or just pushed to the side. Perhaps the conversation seems too often to be revolving around the superintelligence and its threats because that is more sensational—or it sells more—without really making a premise on whether or not the singularity would be even possible. I think this debate is more philosophical than practical, and we shouldn't be too concerned about it.

Professor Fudano goes on to explain that we shall focus on problems that technology makes possible today. For example, we know today that time travel is not feasible. So, the moral dilemmas related to time travel might be right for fictional debates, not for today's practical discussions.

What I love about Fudano's online course is its pragmatism. There aren't too many big, hairy, fancy statements and aspirations. Yet, it covers the issues of applied ethics in AI thoroughly. It gives engineers a solid ethical foundation.

When I was invited to talk about AI in the insurance sector trade shows, I was a contrarian because I voiced my skepticism about superintelligence problems. I could see mixed reactions. The more business-focused audiences could connect with me. They were happy somebody was bringing the conversation about AI down to Earth. Others—mostly those who attended conferences just for some entertainment and a nice day off work—felt a little disappointed.

I often pointed out that we should focus on current issues. For instance, back in 2016, insurance companies struggled to do simple exploratory statistics to better understand their customers' experience. Why should they bother with super-intelligent AI applications when such problems still exist?

THE MAKING OF NEW POSSIBILITIES

We have examined previously some of the new possibilities AI concretizes today, and although I mentioned some trends that made AI possible when we went through its history, we can dive a bit deeper into the progress made in this field that was not possible until recently.

Three broader technological inventions converged into modern AI's success.

The **first** profound technology breakthrough was the internet. AI could not have developed with the telephone or the radio. The internet not only improved communication massively but made it computable as well. In other words, we could record and store data about any activity that happens on the web.

The **second** invention transformed the early internet into the internet that we know today. This novelty was the *HTTP cookie*, a small piece of data stored on your computer by your browser while visiting a website.

Cookies are little packets of data a computer program receives and posts back unchanged. The software engineer Lou Montulli was the first to think of using cookies in web communication in June 1994, when he was working for Netscape Communications (Schwartz, 2001). Netscape introduced cookies as a reliable device for websites to remember preceding events or user interactions such as items added in an online retail store's shopping cart. Today, cookies record the user's whole browsing activity, including clicks on particular buttons, log-in details, browsing history, names, email addresses, credit card numbers, and so on.

The **third**, incredibly transformative technological development was the success of the smartphone. This was due to Apple launching the iPhone in 2007, the first smartphone that worked well. Most importantly, it allowed developers to build applications and publish them on the App Store, creating entirely new economies. This paradigm shift also gave rise to wearable technologies, such as smart watches connected to the internet, which collected even more data.

Before smartphones, people used the internet only on a desktop computer for specific tasks like researching, shopping, or sending emails, and only for a few hours a day. The iPhone's launch marked the era where people plugged into the internet and continuously consumed web services. And to this day they're still plugged in!

So, the internet, web cookies, and smartphones gave birth to the first ingredient that helped AI function properly, namely the generation of an immense amount of data. On the other hand, faster and constant web products and services generated the use cases for AI to grow and no longer be an academic endeavor as you saw when I described the origins of AI. But it set to transform how people consume almost every service today.

An important insight to underline about the development of AI is its speed. Professor Jonathan Haidt helped me notice how significant this is. I was lucky to have the chance to speak with Haidt shortly after I came across his work on moral psychology. He is a notable American social psychologist, professor of ethical leadership at New York University Stern School of Business, and author. His main areas of study are the psychology of morality and moral emotions.

He made a point that stuck with me: "New technologies are often disruptive. Human beings can change enormously, but there is a speed limit. So human societies adapted to electricity, railroads, automobiles, computers, and the internet. And there were often disruptions along the way. But when change is spread out over several decades, it is much less disruptive than if it happens over just several years."

SHOULD WE EVEN DO IT?

In 2016, I was part of a startup accelerator. This program helps entrepreneurs launch their startup through formal teaching, mentorship, and a little seed money. One night, there was a talk from an accomplished entrepreneur, who explained his latest venture's journey. He said something that stuck with me and partly drove me to write this book.

The entrepreneur founded a company that builds technology that helps insurance companies using real-time positioning data from drivers offer motor insurance products based on how well someone drives.

The founder introduced the talk by stating that if something can be done, it is just a matter of time until someone does it. So, you'd better be the first one to seize the opportunity if you want to take advantage of a new possibility. When the iPhone was launched, he realized that everyone had a tracking device continuously plugged into the internet and always in their pocket. The obvious consequence is that you can build connected technology services out of tracking people in real-time.

While that business developed an incredibly positive use case of AI because it directly helps make roads safer, hence saving lives, let us consider the possibility of tracking people in general.

This is the perfect example of something that wasn't possible a few years ago. Now it is, and tracking people raises material moral dilemmas. Is it the right thing to do? Can an organization get away with the user's consent? Internet users gave their permission to be continuously tracked since Netscape created the web cookie, but how conscious are we about the extent to which the internet knows about us? And are we fully aware of how companies use our data?

In the business world, many believe that if we can do something, one has to do it no matter what. Otherwise, others will take advantage of it, and you'll lose your chance to make money out of an idea. While this isn't an aspirational moral compass, I have plenty of experiences where I met people taking it for granted.

One episode was when I was taking the first exploratory phone calls for selling a software implementation to a large insurance company. A member of the Customer Experience and Digital Channel at some point asked me: "Can you automatically scrape Facebook profile data like people's age, gender, locations, likes, preferences, and group memberships?" And I replied with, "What do you need this data for?" And the answer was, "Oh, obviously we use this data to up-sell, cross-sell products, and calibrate the price of the premium." At that point I asked, "Would your customers give their consent for this and would they be properly informed you want to do this?" Unsurprisingly, they told me, "Well, we do this already manually without asking, and not only with our customers but with anybody who looks like a prospect. We just want to find a more efficient way to do it." At that point, the conversation was over. I explained that we found that suggestion unethical, and that as a software vendor, we held our clients to high ethical standards, so we could not go ahead with the project.

What sounds like relatively simple logic isn't straightforward for everybody. For instance, anyone has the faculty and the possibility to harm someone else. Sometimes, the economic (or other) advantage for doing so is even apparent. Think, for example, of defaming a colleague to get a promotion. However, we should not go ahead with something simply because we can do it. We are not like machines, and the way we choose to pursue objectives has to take into account many, many factors. Our immediate convenience is usually a bad and limited one.

The question is often, should we even do this or not? Some consequences and impacts unfortunately become clear only with hindsight. It is very difficult to predict everything that could go wrong with a system. As Professor Pascale Fung recommended when I spoke with her, we shall often let the systems out in the wild to learn what they can do. As Fudano taught us, ethics is born out of the possible. Sometimes, we discover what's possible by trying.

Fung is a renowned computer science professor at the Hong Kong University of Science and Technology. Many like her because she is outspoken, sharp, and energetic. Among the many research streams she has pioneered and contributed to over the years are *chatbots*. These are computer programs that chat automatically with you. Famous ones that you may have interacted with are Siri, Alexa, and the Google Assistant. Others exist in text form. For instance, my first startup developed Zara, a chatbot that insurance company Zurich uses in the UK for helping clients submit claims.

One of the top venues where scientists share their work and publish papers about natural language processing is the annual conference of the Association of Computational Linguistics (ACL). In 2019, ACL was hosted in my home country and, luckily, in my favorite city—Florence. Fung was invited to give the talk "Loquentes Machinae: Technology, Applications, and Ethics of Conversational Systems" (ACL 2019, 2020).

I turned to Pascale Fung for speaking about ethical issues, especially because she was developing CAiRE, a tool similar to the chatbot Replika that we met in earlier chapters (CAiRE, 2021). CAiRE is an "empathetic chatbot" that uses advanced ML algorithms to detect emotions and generate empathetic responses.

Given her vast knowledge of the field, I asked Professor Fung about a recent trend of academic groups (some spun off of companies) developing chatbots as therapists—*Woebot* is such an example (Molteni, 2017). How isn't this creepy? She made three important points that are worth elaborating further for ethical guidelines.

First, "If machines don't make mistakes, it is hard to have guideline and governance. You can build test sets, but there will always be tests you didn't think through."

Provided a system doesn't cause or have a significant risk to cause obvious harm, we shall let the systems play out in the wild to be able to observe misbehavior. We shouldn't be afraid to put systems in production and design appropriate feedback loops to address problems. For instance, on the CAiRE page, you see a "Report" button on the bottom to flag any ethical issues encountered during the conversation with the chatbot. By clicking on it, the conversation log gets sent to the developers, who can intervene on the issue.

The second point she made was about the call for regulation in research. I asked whether we should regulate research on AI, and her take was that if we are speaking about consumer products, "You need to certify a consumer product, like safety issues. I believe there should be third party agencies that should certify that."

From a purely research side, regulation would be too cumbersome for the researcher. Academic bureaucracy like the IRB is already taking too much time off the research work.[4] "What can you regulate? The self-regulating process is the peer review," Prof. Fung says. In fact, before publishing, academic research usually goes through blind reviews from three or more experts in the field of the publication. The peer reviewers also flag ethical concerns, and publication venues like conferences and journals already have robust ethical guidelines and policies in place. It isn't a perfect world, but it is still certainly more advanced.

A key point for Fung is that communication is key. There must be clear, transparent, and honest communication between the system makers and their users. She suggests looking at the example of the Chinese AI policy. It is a comprehensive document outlining the strategy for developing AI in China, including ethical principles to follow and governance (China State Council, 2017).

Finally, she stressed that technical discussions seem to not be engaging on a crucial theme: "should we even be using the system?" Certainly, letting the systems operate out in the wild is helpful to find out their limitations and undesired effects. But a feedback loop shall be designed to make sure there is enough governance, transparency, and a process to take action quickly when users or other stakeholders point out tough feedback.

A piece by the *MIT Technology Review* suggests we should ditch policing computer programs (Heaven, 2020). The article goes over a thorough analysis of case studies like COMPAS (the predictive recidivism system we met earlier) in other parts of the world. On one side, the technicians have an optimistic view: algorithms could be fairer than humans. On the other side, algorithms are fed by biased data, and they amplify that bias, so the solution turns out to be worse than the problem.

I am not sure if an algorithm can really be fairer than a human person, or if removing bias from humans and from reality is even possible.

Most of the moral problems belong to the area of algorithmic and data bias, as we have seen earlier in the case studies. For other examples mentioned throughout this book, we have moral problems with products designed to pursue market or economic goals that generate disastrous side effects. Most of the common action by nonprofits, governments, and academics focus on algorithmic bias.

Again, we meet Ansgar Koene, as he happens to have been part of the research team of project UnBias. Started in 2016 and funded by the EPSRC, UnBias aimed at understanding the concerns and perspectives of the general public when it comes to algorithmic biases. The findings were then used to produce policy recommendations, ethical guidelines, and educational material (UnBias, 2020).

Ansgar told me, "The core issue of using these technologies is the actual aim. So, the focus of ethics would be the people developing these tools. In the majority of big issues, the actual problem was the target that was chosen. Take for example the assessment of who makes the Medicaid cut in the US. The goal was 'how do we reduce the expenses of Medicaid,' so it found how not to qualify people."

"The other problem is when there is a discrepancy between what the algorithm was built for and what people wanted the algorithm to do. When assessing UK A-levels, should the algorithm focus on individual student ability or school performance? The algorithm wanted to make sure the overall grade at a school was not better than the previous year. The actual target was different from what people wanted."

Ansgar wisely added that the topic of ethics goes far beyond AI ethics. EU Commission bureaucrats point out that if we're serious about trust in AI, we need to move away from the you-can-do-it-go-ahead narrative. If we invest because of the "potential" of an application, there are often arguments for not investing in it. For example, we still haven't seen the potential of the promises built on hype such as "AI will solve the big problems, like finding a cure for cancer."

On the economical consideration of AI systems currently deployed in production, Ansgar candidly stated, "Maybe we should work backwards from the problem. Rather than 'we have to be a leader in AI,' [we should recognize] that AI isn't the solution to everything. Being more efficient does not necessarily boost the GDP."

However, we have several examples of applications that went wrong, and it would be the advisable course of action simply to shut them down.

For the majority of new technologies' applications, one cannot predict what can go wrong. Some reveal problems on the way, and chatbots are typically built for noble purposes, but at some point, their severe limitations are revealed.

THE DATA PHILOSOPHER

I interviewed an entrepreneur who made ethics in data and AI his career by knowing more about his work over the years on our topics. I met Charles Radclyffe for the first time in 2016 at a startup accelerator. He made an immediate impression when he handed me a professional looking business card displaying an original job title: "Data Philosopher."

Charles built and sold three tech companies. In between, he has consulted for large financial services organizations on emerging technology. He recently founded EthicsGrade, an ESG benchmarking and ratings agency specializing in the best-practice of technology governance, particularly AI ethics. Outside his day job, Charles advises organizations on how to develop a strategy of ethical implementation of AI, automation, and robotics (as well as speaking at events on this subject), co-hosts a soon-to-be-released podcast, and writes a blog on the ethics and societal impact of emerging technology. Charles holds an MA in Law from Cambridge, and he is a fan of science fiction and early modern history.

Charles' story is very interesting. With his third company, they were competing for a bid for a company they were feeling a bit edgy about. Luckily, they lost the bid because the prospect ended up having reputational problems. This organization's engineers were truly talented and interested in undeniably complex problems and clever solutions. However, what they couldn't see was the impact, the ripple effect, that the tech they were building had.

He also worked on a project with a large bank. Again, his team felt they shouldn't be doing it. Many of the client's techies were excited to develop tools that were ethically questionable. When Radclyffe's team raised their reservations with the project's sponsor, she said, "Focus on the year end targets, don't worry about the fluffy stuff."

Many businesses unfortunately see things like ethical policies and conduct, social responsibility, and equity in the workplace as the "fluffy stuff." For them, what really drives decisions is the short-term profit.

Charles also gave me the example of a very positive business that does things differently. Fidelity Investments is a large American asset management firm. It is owned by a family, and Abigail Johnson, its president and chief executive officer since 2014, cares about the reputation of her family and company. When Charles worked with them, they explained to him that when they were thinking about governance, they assumed naively to hire big consulting firms so they could tell them what to do. What the big consulting firms proposed to Fidelity was: 1) how they can manage to stay compliant and 2) how they can implement good engineering standards (manage the risk). But the question the team at Fidelity was asking was different. They asked: "How do we not cross the 'creepy line?' How do we preserve our reputation? We asked the tech companies themselves. We were big investors in Alibaba, Google, Amazon, Microsoft, IBM, Apple. They did a lot of work on AI ethics. But what we got was more of the same: engineering practices to manage the risk. Again, we could not get a good answer."

Charles went on to explain where his team's approach differed:

"European AI governance standards require us to be 'lawful, ethical, and robust.' Risk management is about robustness (bias and fairness can be solved by engineering efforts). Lawfulness is regulatory compliance (lots of firms weren't good with GDPR) and to be involved in the design of the regulation (encourage regulation). How do you not cross the creepy line (very different types of problems) is about ethics. This regards how well a business consulted the stakeholders and how well they implemented the feedback loop with stakeholders, and how well they communicated."

This feedback loop is crucial. Nothing is set in stone—products and customer needs keep changing. With technology today, this feedback loop became ever so faster. Governance for the loop, dynamic and timely response to stakeholders, and impeccable communication are key ingredients for doing the right thing (Radclyffe and Nodell, 2020).

I was interested to know more about when wider economic goals clash with customers' well-being, an issue many AI-driven products share. I asked Charles if there is a conflict between profit making and customer interests. For example, YouTube maximizes time spent on the platform, and the algorithms responsible for achieving this goal end up creating polarization, rabbit holes, and incite extremism.

He explained, starting with a quick historical perspective. In the nineteenth century, individual entrepreneurs built enormous wealth with industrialization. It was the age of Rockefeller, the individual capitalist. The twentieth century was the shareholder century. It was really about professional managers, leaders running corporations in order to maximize shareholder value. The twenty-first century saw the idea of twentieth century leaders upgraded by technology. Technology could be much more effective than any previous method, but the approach became unsustainable. The younger generation is much more interested in stakeholders than shareholders (how your supply chain is managed, the environment, the community).

We're seeing a big shift. In the twenty-first century, stakeholder value has become more important.

I could relate to this change through personal experience. Freshly out of college, when I started applying for jobs, I could see interviews were all about shareholder returns. I was pitched companies on short-term goals like share price, client success, quarterly targets, etc. When I started hiring people for my startup, I could see this young generation probing about our startup mission, our team values. And when I explained to them that we couldn't offer as much money as the big corporations offered them, they didn't care. They were looking for meaningful work, a human-centered team who cared for them and their stakeholders as people, rather than numbers. Finally, when I recently interviewed for Tesla, I could clearly see a big contrast with the experience I had in my early career. When I asked people why they liked it there, nobody mentioned targets, money, or the share price which made many employees millionaires between 2019 and 2020. The united answer was "to accelerate the transition to cleaner energy."

There is no perfect balance between making money and doing good by society. Hopefully, we find a somewhat balanced approach that works. Capitalism is good for incentivizing risk taking, but not great for disincentivizing doing harm.

Charles made the example of Facebook, which has realized that if they don't do something, they might not exist in a future not far from now. They have turned a lot. Their oversight board (oversightboard.com) is a good example of a feedback mechanism, but it is quite narrow. While users have standing, they only do so for content decisions and not for wider questions about Facebook or Instagram's business model. It is quite limited in terms of scope, and it is too early to say if it will have success. Radclyffe made one more small example: urban planning and design. "We understand what success looks like—you ask everyone about their needs, then when we deliver the project, everyone feels they contributed. The big difference between urban space and Facebook is that the former has three million users, the latter three billion. The challenge is finding a way everyone feels they were included." Charles is not yet convinced Facebook will make it.

THE CASE FOR REGULATION

I then discussed with him if the solution can only be more regulation.

"In our podcast, *Are You a Robot?*, we interviewed Harriet Moore, science fiction writer. Moore asked, 'Does it really matter if we slow down innovation a little bit?' In 1989, Tim Barnes Lee invented the WWW. In 1995, Netscape invented the cookie. It was the cookie that made the world as we live today. It was only in 2011 that we started realizing that we should regulate personal data in the EU. In 2016, it became law. In 2018 it was implemented. Regulation is too slow. We need more agility, and the power of lobbies is too strong. The tech industry spends far too much on lobbying. If there is one thing I'd regulate, it would be this: when Zuckerberg, Bezos, etc. [were asked] 'Is Amazon a monopoly?' the question was the wrong one to ask.

"I started my career in finance. In 2005 to 2006, the popular question was whether Leman Brother was a monopoly. After 2008, everyone realized the right question was: "Was LB really too big to fail?" So, the question would be which companies would be too big to fail in tech? Amazon and WhatsApp are too big to fail. If we had smaller tech companies, we'd have more innovation."

Yes, regulation could be slow, but it can also be the opportunity to slow down. When asking the same question to Jonathan Haidt, he expanded on his point on technologies developing at too fast of a pace. One argument for regulation, Haidt believes, is that "slowing things down, giving time for people to adapt—giving time for social institutions and politics to adapt—is maybe a good thing in itself, given how powerful and how disruptive this technology could be."

As we previously drew a parallel between marketing and AI for their power to influence behavior, Haidt noted that development speed is again essential. "Marketing developed over many decades, actually, in the 1920s and on, in a consumer society. There have been regulations, laws about false advertising, and laws that prevent companies from marketing to children."

Haidt recalled that when he was young, lawyers and drug companies could not advertise on television. Still, cigarette companies could do so. In the late twentieth century, all three of those laws were reversed, so marketing is regulated and has always been. Haidt added: "But I would also say that marketing does not have the potential to disrupt society the way that artificial intelligence or nuclear power does. I would think of AI more like nuclear power than like wind energy. I'm sure there are regulations on wind energy, but we're generally much more careful, and we make [many] more regulations on nuclear power because of its vast potential both for good and for evil."

ETHICAL FOUNDATIONS

As Radclyffe described himself as the data philosopher, I had to ask him a philosophical question: "Is it possible to agree on a common shared truth?"

He gave a very practical answer: "The assumption is in some way, you have to find a principle. This is really hard; we probably can't do this. Perhaps, you don't need to. Instead, one can work out a mechanism to be rigorous in their thinking and reasonable with their stakeholders. While most people would say or recognize that an organization is behaving ethically, the problem the organization is trying to solve is reputation. A major British bank, for instance, was infamous for tracking employees' behavior based on keyboard typing and mouse movements. They would surveil if they were working or not. These things don't happen if a company has a rigorous procedure. Ethics is about acting. Using a sport metaphor, it is not about the rules of the game, but how you play." Radclyffe added that setting up ethical frameworks in companies often result in writing down core values such as "we believe in actions, we care deeply about integrity, hard work, etc." and they don't connect these concepts with policies, protocols, and robust governance.

"The truth is a continuous process, not set in stone. It requires building bottom up, not top down." Charles concluded our chat with a quote by William James:

"There is no such thing possible as an ethical philosophy dogmatically made up in advance.... There can be no final truth in ethics any more than in physics, until the last man has had his experience and his say" (James, 1956).

Figuring out where to start and focusing on what ethical framework to implement is very complex. We have learned that new possibilities introduce new moral choices. We have seen many technologies that AI made possible and that are already operating in the real world. These technologies present issues such as reasoning whether or not something should be done, and who should be responsible for making sure these applications don't remain unchecked. Professionals like Koene and Radclyffe are pushing forward viable solutions, and luckily, they are not alone.

While I leave the debates about superintelligence or general artificial intelligence to the world of fantasy, we have seen how science fiction could help. Its fictional elements permit us to detach from the current world and our political views, moving lightheartedly into new worlds. In these stories, we could find the starting point underneath everything that concerns ethical problems with the latest technology. Earlier we explored sci-fi movies that introduced themes like our awareness of ourselves, the relationships between people, people and technology, power, and the economy. How to live together and live a fulfilling life. Science fiction helped us picture future scenarios and offered the first step into the profound questions that intrigue humanity.

I asked Haidt if we have to start from an anthropological model for speaking of the ethics of AI, and he confirmed that this is indeed very important, in a way, disagreeing with William James' quote above:

"Yes, I'm very confident of this and that you need to create a psychologically realistic AI ethics. It is sometimes said that you cannot derive an 'ought' from an 'is' (CFR Jenkins (2017)), but in fact, I believe you can only derive 'ought' statements from 'is' statements. I mean only if you know what kinds of creatures we are and how we live together. Only after you have a description of human beings and human morality, including all its variations, can you begin to make normative statements. That is what we ought to do."

The question that is at the heart of the ethical problem is who we think the human person is.

"*AI wants only the genuine article:* machines with minds, *in the full and literal sense. This is not science fiction, but real science, based on a theoretical conception as deep as it is daring: namely, we are, at root,* computers ourselves."

—JOHN HAUGELAND IN *ARTIFICIAL INTELLIGENCE: THE VERY IDEA*

CHAPTER 8

What Is Human: Part I

Defining humanity is no easy feat.

In the science fiction psychological thriller *Ex Machina* (2014), Caleb is a programmer invited by his CEO to administer the Turing Test to an intelligent humanoid robot. The robot seems so convincingly human that Caleb, at some point, is no longer able to distinguish reality from appearance. He can no longer be sure if he is a human being.

It is, however, necessary to dive into the problem of defining humanity in order to adequately frame the problems we have seen so far and lay down the foundation for developing AI ethically.

Science fiction has been responsible for overhyping and, to a certain extent, has influenced the public perception and understanding of AI. However, its most significant merit is to challenge us to ask profound questions. And one critical question is whether or not we, as philosopher John Haugeland puts it succinctly, are computers ourselves.

Many of the common concerns people express over advancements in AI seem to stem from the same thing—the fear that, deep down, humans are no different from machines.

Philosophers have struggled to define humanity for centuries. What is it that makes us human? What makes us unique?

I don't feel qualified, nor is it the aim of this book, to answer these questions, but I can point out a few functional elements of humanity to help distinguish man from machine. Asking who or what the human person is helps us reach a necessary starting point for deciding how to implement a technology that profoundly affects humanity. AI applications are defined by their purpose in relationship with their users—human persons.

ABILITY TO MAKE UP NARRATIVES

When researching what modern thinkers say about the human being's nature, I came across some influential historians in tech circles.

The historians are Y. N. Harari, author of *Homo Sapiens: A Brief History of Humankind* (2014) and *Homo Deus: A Brief History of Tomorrow (2018)*, and R. Potts and C. Sloan, the authors of *What Does it Mean to Be Human?* (2010). Harari, Potts, and Sloan explain that about seventy thousand years ago, organisms belonging to the Homo sapiens species started forming complex structures called *culture*. The following development of human cultures is called *history*.

According to these historians, what started history is something they define as the *cognitive revolution*. This is the process whereby humans started having new ways of thinking and communicating. The first noticeable feature of human language (in fact, language existed in other animal species) was the ability to tell stories—in particular, to make up narratives about characters and objects that don't necessarily exist.

Harari argues that this ability to construct powerful narratives is what made humans able to cooperate and distinguish themselves from other species. Cultural evolution takes the place of genetic change. Human reality can no longer be explainable only by chemistry, biology, or physics.

Harari doesn't give a definition of the human person. While in his writings he seems to embrace an evolutionary view of the human person (humans are the sum of their evolutionary steps) and a little of the Cartesian view that humans are defined by their capacity to think, he seems to recognize that human nature isn't mechanically made up of biology and cultural heritage alone. Humans are something more. Harari tries to explain this something more as humans' ability to craft powerful stories.

COGITO ERGO SUM

One of the philosophical definitions of the human being that primarily influenced modern science is the famous *cogito ergo sum* deducted by René Descartes. In fact, we've met him already when speaking about the philosophical foundations of AI. It's not by chance that the science fiction movie *The*

13th floor, which is about sentient computer programs and simulated realities, begins with Descartes' famous quote.

Descartes systematized the scientific and philosophical conceptions that started in the Renaissance and culminated with Modernity. Werner Heisenberg—one of the fathers of modern physics, who codified the principles of quantum mechanics—explains the limits of Descartes' work in in a great philosophical compendium of modern science (Heisenberg, 2007). The key finding of quantum mechanics, the indetermination principle, states that you cannot know position and speed of an elementary particle at the same time, because once you decide to measure one quantity, the act of measuring it modifies the other. The human measure interferes with the reality itself, making it knowable to humans only in relationship with their measurement device.

In essence, modern physics shows the impossibility of a net separation between the world and the "I."

The problem of Descartes' philosophy is the separation between "res cogitans"—the realm of thought, the spirit, or soul—and "res extensa"—the reality of the body, the organic and inorganic matter.

Descartes was obliged to put animals and plants in the world of "rex extensa." Plants and animals were not essentially different from machines, and their behaviors were entirely determined by material causes. It follows that if animals were considered merely as machines, it was difficult not to think the same about humans. One of the sensational discoveries of modern physics is that natural science doesn't only describe and explain nature. It is an inherent part of the reciprocal action between us and nature. It represents nature in relationship with the systems (measures) used by scientists for studying it.

The human person reduced only to its capacity of thinking, or rationalizing things, led to the terrible simplification economists made about human nature.

THE *HOMO ECONOMICUS*
Modern Neoclassical economic theory assumes that the human person is rational. Stigler (1987) concisely formalizes the hypothesis underlying modern economic thinking:

"There are three characteristics of a rational consumer:

1. His tastes are consistent.
2. His cost calculations are correct.
3. He makes those decisions that maximize utility."

Although many classical economists like Smith, Malthus, and Ricardo recognize that people are in reality irrational, subject to emotions and moved by other motives, economics needed a formalization that would be suitable for writing mathematical equations and demonstrating principles because it was developing into a science (McCormick, 1997). McCormick states, on this regard:

"In order to apply mathematics to consumer behavior, one *must* assume a certain predictable regularity of behavior."

To get a better understanding of the most recent evolutions of philosophy and the topics we're exploring, I turned to Professor Michele Averchi. He is an associate professor at the Catholic University of America. His research focuses on Husserlian phenomenology and early phenomenology (in particular Max Scheler and Maritz Geiger) with a strong interest in the phenomenology of the self. His most recent work is on the phenomenology of communication and knowledge-sharing.

Averchi attended the same university I went to in Milan, but I didn't know much of him at the time. He graduated with a degree in philosophy while I was just starting with physics. He's the twin brother of a physicist who helped me prepare for the exam of Optics. Both twins are geniuses in their fields. Michele has a profound knowledge of modern philosophy and can explain complicated concepts with simplicity. This is often the case when someone knows and understands their subject very well. It is a pleasure speaking with him, especially as he speaks calmly with a warm tone and funny French "R."

When I asked him about the human person's truth, ethics, and moral decisions, Michele said that everyone has to start from an anthropological model. Some may say that you don't need one for establishing a set of moral norms or a code of ethics. In reality, even the ones who say so are implicitly making an assumption of what the human person is. Say a group of people working at the same company consider which behavior they can use to influence their customers to make more money. They are likely making an implicit assumption like the *Homo economicus* model, i.e., human persons are modeled as rational beings moved by the optimization of their utility. This is often modeled into a so-called "utility function." The business has to play with this model to extract as much money as possible.

I believe many of the examples of AI applications we have seen leading to despicable outcomes come from this view of humanity.

CARING FOR THE TRUTH

I then asked Averchi whether modern thinking cares about answering the human person's question, or whether given that we cannot agree on such a sensitive topic, we shall give up on it. I was curious to understand if there was still an interest in seeking the truth in a society where posing specific questions risks slipping into the politically incorrect discourse.

Averchi explained to me that, first and foremost, philosophers always believed in the truth. No philosopher has really negated the existence of the truth. Perhaps they cast doubts about an absolute truth, but there is a truth in a context or a horizon. The question is whether there is a horizon. Discussions on these points, when translated by the media or more popular publications, risk becoming shallow and may lead people to believe that nobody cares about the truth. Or that the discourse on the truth is too uncomfortable. Suddenly, something happens that strikes a chord—for example, something with political or economic relevance. Then the truth starts becoming attractive again. For instance, when fake news started being fabricated for political influence and for manipulating consumers, you have *The New York Times'* first brand campaign in a decade saying, "Truth. It's more important now than ever" (*The New York Times*, 2017).

Averchi suggested that I take a look at philosophers Hubert Dreyfus, John Haugeland, and Robert Sokolowski, who ask the important questions about human nature as well as artificial intelligence.

HUMANS CARE

We have seen with Heisenberg that humans cannot be detached from their context. Mind and body are interconnected and influence each other. Contrasting humans and machines, Dreyfus explains the relationship with context.

In *Mind Over Machine* (1986), written during the heyday of expert systems, Dreyfus analyzed the difference between human expertise and the programs that claimed to capture it. This expanded on ideas from *What Computers Can't Do*, where he had made a similar argument criticizing the "cognitive simulation" school of AI research practiced by Allen Newell and Herbert A. Simon in the 1960s (Dreyfus, 1972). Dreyfus argued that human problem-solving and expertise depend on our background sense of the context of what is essential and exciting given the situation, rather than on the process of searching through combinations of possibilities to find what we need. Dreyfus would describe it in 1986 as the difference between "knowing-that" and "knowing-how," based on Heidegger's distinction of present-at-hand and ready-to-hand.

One of the things we observed in earlier chapters about AI and its applications is that the machine struggles to adapt to new contexts. In contrast, the human person has an incredible ability to adapt and face new situations because it is able to pull from prior experiences to better establish itself.

Haugeland, in a 1979 book about AI, suggests, "The trouble with artificial intelligence is that computers don't give a damn." We are different from machines because we care, we seek the meaning, and use reason as an openness to know the world and explain it. Our thirst for purpose could be the hidden link between the context, our understanding of it, and the ability to adapt.

Debating with Averchi, he suggested that this capacity for caring for the human species underlies a critical difference between Harari's anthropology and Dreyfus' and Haugeland's. As a historian, Harari might not explain why people create stories. Still, he seems to hint that this emerged as an innovative strategy for making large groups of humans collaborate, hence winning the evolutionary fight for survival. However, it is more reasonable to say that humans make up stories first and foremost to find meaning, explain reality, and pass on traditions to posterity. The point is not really whether these stories are true or false, but that they attempt to describe a meaning. Insofar as these stories correspond to the desire for justice and truth, they gain traction and pull together people to collaborate.

So, fear not, it doesn't look like humans are like machines. I want to complete this journey of laying down the foundations of humanity by introducing in the next chapter an author whose work changed my life.

This is where I learned that we have in ourselves a criterion to confront any given situation, which is the key ingredient that humanity has in order to behave morally.

"There will be little rubs and disappointments everywhere, and we are all apt to expect too much; but then, if one scheme of happiness fails, human nature turns to another; if the first calculation is wrong, we make a second better: we find comfort somewhere."

—JANE AUSTEN IN MANSFIELD PARK

CHAPTER 9

What Is Human: Part II

Why do you care?

In our quest for defining humanity, we have seen that humans adapt to an enormous number of situations. We can figure our way out of an incredible number of circumstances. We are also creatures who care for knowing the truth. We care for relationships. We care for things being right and just. We care that things are beautiful. We care about many profound things. We have this inner strength that is difficult to name.

When I was fourteen years old, a high school friend gave me a book by Luigi Giussani, an Italian priest and educator with a passion for answering life's greatest mysteries. I fell in love with his work and the bold approach to his work on education. I was deeply impressed by this man who was not afraid to elicit and face the deep questions that come up when we are young and accompany us for the rest of our lives—why are we here? What is the purpose of our life?

As my logical brain started developing, I felt drawn to math, physics, and natural sciences, I loved how the way Father

Giussani wrote and spoke was like a true scientist. His logic was impeccable.

Giussani's work, *The Religious Sense* (1997), is a simple, easily digestible handbook for understanding humanity and those questions that fall into the human experience's spiritual realm. His work in describing this side of humanity is founded on three essential premises: realism, reasonableness, and morality in action.

REALISM

Realism is letting the object of scrutiny suggest the method for knowing it. Take, for example, a toddler toying around with a smartphone for the first time. Most parents can attest that when their children first discovered their phones, they did anything they could to try and destroy them. But this destruction is not intentional. Instead, it is the child's attempt to try and understand how to use the item they are holding. If there is an on button, that must do something, right? Let's press it. It is the object that "suggests" how to discover it and eventually use it.

Defining humanity requires an existential inquiry, similarly to Giussani's attempt in his work to talk about the religious experience. Giussani points out that when it comes to essential questions, we have to find the answer ourselves. He notes that either consciously or unconsciously, most people would trust the words of others for understanding something important like our own spiritual experience. But would it be correct to study what Aristotle, Plato, Kant, Marx, or Engels say about it? Giussani answers by underlying the concept of using realism for such an important quest:

"We could do this, but, as a first step, the method would be incorrect. When we deal with this fundamental expression of man's existence, we simply cannot abandon ourselves to the opinions of others, absorbing the most fashionable views or impressions that determine our milieu. Realism requires a certain method for observing and coming to know an object, and this method must not be imagined, thought of or organized and created by the subject: it must be imposed *by the object*" (Giussani, 1997).

Using realism to understand the depth of the human person means we shall start with an existential inquiry about ourselves. What do we know about ourselves? What experience do we have about our inner selves?

"If I did not begin with this existential inquiry, it would be like asking someone else to define a phenomenon that I experience. This external consultation must confirm, enrich, or contest the fruits of my own personal reflection. Otherwise, I would be substituting the opinion of others for a task that belongs to me, and, in the end, I would form an inevitably alienating opinion. I would be uncritically adopting from others a conception regarding a problem important for my life and my destiny."

Here, a concept that is important to understand further is the word *experience*. When I spoke earlier about machine vs. human learning, I mentioned how human experience is not as automated as ingesting information or a mere trial and error.

Taking one step further, it is helpful to take a look at the original way Giussani talks about human experience: "The word 'experience' does not mean exclusively 'to try': the man of experience is not one who has accumulated 'experiences'—facts and sensations—and has lumped them all together. Such an indiscriminate accumulation often destroys and empties the personality. Experience certainly means 'trying' something, but primarily it also coincides with a judgment we make about what we try. . . . Above all, the person is self-awareness. Thus, what characterizes experience is not so much action, that is, mechanically establishing relations with reality: what defines experience is *understanding* something, discovering its meaning. Thus experience implies understanding the meaning of things. A judgment requires a *criterion* on the basis of which the judgment can be made."

We come back to wisdom. It is up to humans to be wise. There are two alternatives for *understanding something*: either borrow the criterion from the outside, or the measure lies within yourself. The problem with the first possibility would be to slip again into the alienating situation described earlier. If you undertake an existential inquiry, you could choose if you want someone else to explain to you what you find and experience within the depth of your heart. The meaning of your experience would depend on something outside of yourself. Otherwise, a reasonable, non-alienating alternative would be to find within ourselves, within our human structure, the criterion for judging the reflection of an existential inquiry.

Giussani defines the criterion using the words *elementary experience*.

The elementary experience "can be described as a complex of needs and 'evidence' which accompany us as we come face to face with all that exists. Nature thrusts man into a universal comparison with himself, with others, with things, and furnishes him with a complex of original needs and 'evidences,' which are tools for that encounter. So original are these needs or these 'evidences' that everything man does or says depends on them. These needs can be given many names. They can be summarized with different expressions (for example, the need for happiness, the need for truth, for justice, etc.). They are like a spark igniting the human motor."

We have an innate desire for happiness, for truth, justice, freedom, beauty, etc. This desire is the ultimate judge of our experience. Haugeland underlines that humans care. In fact, the dis-humanity of autonomous decision systems is precisely that computers do not care about a decision being just, proper, or something that brings happiness to the user.

Using realism invites us to use things for what they are. If humans are like machines, nothing stops us from treating them like machines. If humans are something more, we shall treat them for who they are.

The second premise for better understanding humanity is our need for things to be *reasonable*, which is linked to the pursuit of truth—truth has to be reasonable.

REASONABLENESS

Giussani again uses an original way to speak about reasonableness. He explains that something is reasonable if it takes into account all the facets that define it. According to the Italian educator, *reason* is "the distinctive characteristic of that level of nature that we call man, that is, the capacity to become aware of reality according to the totality of its factors. The term *reasonableness*, then, represents a mode of action that expresses and realizes reason, the capacity to become aware of reality."

While the reason is the capacity to become aware of the reality in all its factors, it can still be used unreasonably, i.e., without adequate motives. Moreover, *reasonable* is also different from *rational*. Rational is usually meant as demonstrable. Giussani points out that "although it is certain that the reasonable seeks, desires, aspires, and is curious to demonstrate everything, it is not true that reasonable is identical with demonstrable: the capacity to demonstrate is an aspect of reasonableness, but the reasonable is not solely the capacity to demonstrate."

In his *Phenomenology of the Human Person* (2008), Sokolowski uses the term the "agent of truth" as a synonym for the human person and for distinguishing human from animal. A classical definition of "human being" was "rational animal." However, Sokolowski points out that the agent of truth has a couple of advantages over the rational animal:

"First, it expands the meaning of thinking and truth. The word 'rational' seems to limit thinking to calculation and inference, but the new phrase does not connote such a restriction. It encompasses all the forms of understanding, including those that go beyond language."

Reasonability becomes even more critical with less "tangible," yet more existential realities like love. I don't need to, and I probably can't, demonstrate with a lab experiment or a logical theorem that my wife loves me. According to Giussani, the truly interesting question for humankind is "neither logic, a fascinating game, nor demonstration, an inviting curiosity. Rather, the intriguing problem . . . is how to adhere to reality, to become aware of reality."

As we've previously discussed, this reason is one of the primary ways that we come to learn about the world around us.

So, Giussani investigates what methodology reason can use to acquire certainty on things like the love of your parents, a partner, or an important person for your life. He notes that while mathematics, the sciences, and philosophy are fundamental conditions for civilization, one could live very well without philosophy or knowing that the Earth revolves around the sun. "Man cannot live, however, without moral certainties, without being able to form sure judgments about the behavior of others toward him."

For Giussani, "to arrive at certainties about relationships we have been given the fastest of methods, almost more like intuition than a process. . . . The method by which I understand that my mother loves me and through which I am certain that many people are my friends cannot be fixed mechanically; my intelligence intuits that the only reasonable meaning, the only reasonable interpretation of the convergence of a given set of 'signs' is this. If these signs, in their hundreds and thousands, could be indefinitely multiplied, their only adequate meaning would be that my mother loves me. Thousands of indications converge on this point: my mother's behavior only means this: 'my mother loves me.'

This is called not just a moral certainty, but also an *existential certainty*, because it is bound to the moment at which you examine the phenomenon, that is, when you intuit all of the signs. An example: I am not worried that the person now in front of me may want to kill me. . . . I reach this conclusion by reading certain facets of his behavior and a specific situation. But I could not be as certain about the future, when the circumstances might be very different" (Giussani, 1997).

MORALITY IN ACTION

Sokolowski (2008) explains the second advantage of defining the human person as the agent of truth instead of a rational animal: "attaining truth is an accomplishment and not merely passive reception. It speaks not just about reasoning but about success in reasoning, and so designates human being in terms of its highest achievement: the human person is defined by being engaged in truth, and human action is based on truth."

Acquiring knowledge, knowing something, is about seeking its truth. This is an action, and morality plays a significant role in this quest.

Overcoming the pitfalls of Descartes' dualistic philosophy, which we've seen when speaking about the origins of AI,

Giussani explains that the human person is one and whole. Different components affect each other and cannot function separately. For example, a student is very good at math and consistently scores at the top of the class. She's a brilliant mind. Say one day, she parties all night. The following day, she has an exam and scores very poorly. Is her brilliant mind no longer working? No, she was simply too tired, and the body affected the capacity of her brain to function at its best. Likewise, feelings are connected. Perhaps she would also score poorly if she had just broken up with her boyfriend.

Feelings are a phenomenon inherent to human beings that we cannot leave out. There is a profound unity between the reason and the rest of the person. The reason isn't like a machine that can be disconnected from the rest of the personality, and it cannot operate alone.

Giussani explains that "these phenomena have a common denominator: something always has an impact on the individual's sphere of experience." He expands on the nature of feelings by making a comparison with a focal lens. The higher the value of something that matters to me, the stronger the emotion that I feel. Emotions are like lenses that help us focus on what matters most and what matters less, though it takes a particular effort to put feelings in an appropriate place. This work is moral decision-making.

Say, for example, a coworker slights you in a meeting. This would probably piss you off, yeah? What would happen if you had to go into another meeting with them later that day? Chances are good that you wouldn't hear a word they say—you'd be too focused on how you're exacting revenge in your fantasies. Instead, you decide to do the right thing and listen to them. This also allows you to look the coworker in their eyes, perhaps recognizing their great idea at the meeting, and work together. This puts both in a better position for resolving the injustice in another moment.

This example resembles a circumstance that has actually happened to me several times at work. It shows how the capacity to learn and act is deeply affected by morality, much more than logical decision-making. Using Giussani's words,

"It seems evident to me . . . that the heart of the problem of human knowledge does not lie in a particular intellectual capacity. The more a value is vital and elementary in its importance—destiny, affection, common life—the more our nature gives to each of us the intelligence to know and judge it. The center of the problem is really a proper position of the heart, a correct attitude, a feeling in its place, a morality."

OVERCOMING THE *HOMO ECONOMICUS*: RESPONSIBILITY

We have previously spoken about the simplistic model of the *Homo economicus*. In this framework, the human person only cares about maximizing their personal gain. Businesses make decisions based on this model. In fact, most commercial applications of AI seem to adhere to this model.

We have seen many examples of how maximizing for the wrong objective created problematic AI applications. Professor Jonathan Haidt, who you met earlier, made an incredibly good point regarding the need to rethink business models that can reflect more human values. He mentioned that while Instagram and Twitter are looking into small things they can do to add friction, these tiny adjustments are not going to really affect their business model:

"But [Instagram, Twitter] are aware of the problems. They are trying to do things like hiding the 'like' counter on Instagram or tagging suspicious posts or untrue posts on Twitter. So, there are undoubtedly some tiny things that they can do.

Typically, in a capitalist economy, products get better and better at serving their customers and not harming their customers. The difficulty here is that the advertisers are the customers in these advertising-driven platforms, more so than the users. One possible solution to put pressure on Facebook is to make more room for alternate kinds of networks that are not driven by advertising revenue. Wikipedia is an excellent example of a different business model. It hasn't made billions of dollars, but it does a huge public service."

When I asked where an attempt to address the ethics of these applications could start from, Haidt suggested drawing heavily on social psychology and looking at the nature of human interactions. For example, we shall look into what contexts can incentivize people to care more about the truth and less about their own prestige.

The same techniques that won Richard Thaler the Nobel Prize, nudging, could be better used in this way.

Haidt proposed that, for example, platforms could incentivize their users to be cooperative, truthful, helpful, and kind. He also noted:

"Facebook and Twitter have taken over the traditional roles of the public square where people talk about issues relevant to them in their town, community, or country. And Twitter, I think, in particular, does it in a way that incentivizes practices that are bad for democracy and bad for good discussion. So, we can certainly talk about healthier or less healthy conversations, and the more exchange involves obscenities and aggression and showing off for your side versus meeting, learning about and understanding other people, the more we can say with confidence that the consequence is wrong or bad for communication."

It is time businesses, governments, and organizations embrace a more encompassing view of humanity. Within ourselves, we tend toward a set of values that guide our choices and go way beyond personal gain.

Moreover, plenty of empirical evidence about our behavior going beyond personal gain exists. One example is mentioned in a brilliant study from Professor Haidt himself. In an experiment, you'd be asked to name the price that someone would have to pay you (anonymously and secretly) to convince you to do a set of ten actions. For each one, you could assume there will be no social, legal, or material consequences.

The actions were five pairs of different variants. For instance, action one was formulated in two options: option A, sticking a pin into your palm; option B, in the palm of a child you don't know. While the first action was concerned with moral principles of harm/care, the other activities regarded other dimensions. Another example would be: option A, slapping a friend in the face (with his/her permission) as part of a comedy skit; option B, slapping your father in the face (with his permission) as part of a comedy skit.

The publication explains that "*Homo economicus* would prefer the option in column B to the option in column A for action 1 and would be more or less indifferent to the other four pairs. In contrast, a person with moral motives would (on average) require a larger payment to engage in the actions in column B and would feel dirty or degraded for engaging in some of these actions for personal enrichment" (Haidt, 2007).

In an extended essay about integral human development and organization of work, economists Russo and Vaccaro share a similar objective as us. As they speak about human work and development, they first define who the human person is because they want to address the development of the person as a whole and update economic models that are no longer sustainable (Russo and Vaccaro, 2013).

It is interesting to find that, starting from an economic reflection, they describe several characteristics of humanity similar to those we highlighted.

First, Russo and Vaccaro point out our inner voice. They remind us that it is sufficient to look within ourselves to understand the peculiarity of the human person compared to other natural beings.

Then, they note that observing that humans are different from animals by nature (by birth) doesn't mean we want to claim "supremacy" over other creatures and dominate them. Instead, it means that the peculiarity of our nature gives us the duty to live according to our human dignity and, hence, to respect the dignity of our fellow humans and look after the environment and other creatures. This task didn't fall on other living beings (like animals or plants). For example, while we condemn the *inhuman* behavior of infanticide, we don't stop to accuse a parasite that infests a plant or a chimpanzee devouring another chimp from a rival herd.

The perception of a task toward our peers, nature, and the environment introduces responsibility. We can only ask accountability of a being that can form relationships, that is free and capable of transcendence. Russo and Vaccaro conclude that men and women don't depend univocally and necessarily on their innate impulses (mechanically, as I was concerned regarding free will when speaking with Fagan). Still, they use them to consciously tend toward an end, an objective.

Human existence can only be understood in its wholeness. Reductions or oversimplifications exclude certain aspects— as Giussani would say, they are not reasonable. Moreover, personal experience shows us that we can experience a certain tension between diverse contexts in life. Still, in the end, we perceive a profound unity in ourselves: for example, think about how the intellectual knowledge of the truth brings us joy, or how a vital choice we make influences our body's reactions (Russo and Vaccaro, 2013).

Giussani's all-encompassing view of the human person gives us a solid framework for moral action. According to Giussani, the human being is that level of nature that becomes aware of itself and cares about being just, being right, and truthful. Humans care about and seek their happiness and self-fulfillment. They need to find reasonable answers, and the way they acquire certainty about something is necessarily impacted by their morality.

Russo and Vaccaro's views introduce critical categories for considering the human person as a whole: responsibility, relationality, freedom, and transcendence.

We now put all of this together for drafting a blueprint for the ethical development of AI.

"*If technical progress is not matched by corresponding progress in man's ethical formation, in man's inner growth, then it is not progress at all, but a threat for man and for the world.*"
—POPE BENEDICT XVI IN *SPE SALVI*

CHAPTER 10

Ethical AI or Ethical Humans?

―

One day, I was on vacation with a group of friends. It was a great mix of nationalities: a couple Italian families, an American one, and a Guinean/British dad with his two kids. We were having dinner at a restaurant in the Meridien resort of Sharja, in the UAE. With many children around, discussions were constantly interrupted by a "why" question, and at some point one kid asked my wife a fantastic question. My wife Laura is a physicist, and her research involves building enormous detectors to observe and discover particles that are so small (smaller than atoms, in fact) they can't be observed with a microscope. Laura is great when explaining complex science to kids, and what she said that night defined the way I think about artificial intelligence.

The child asked, "Why do you build super-duper big tanks of liquid gas to detect tiny particles?"

And my wife said (and I'm paraphrasing here), "When scientists wanted to study something small, they invented the microscope using two lenses. You know how that works, right?"

The kid nodded.

"Then they wanted to study something even smaller, so they improved microscopes by using better lenses, then lasers, then connecting them to a computer, until they could no longer use anything like a microscope for looking at things that are smaller than the particles that make the atoms."

The child's eyes were widening, along with their mouth.

"So, scientists needed to change strategy, and think about something different than the microscope. They realized that if these tiny particles bounce against other particles in liquid gas, we can view a trace they leave, like the cloudy trail space rockets leave behind when you see them flying in the sky. Although we cannot see the particle itself, that trail gives us a lot of information about the particle, like how big it is, what energy it carries, and so on. The tanks are huge because it is so unlikely that a tiny particle interacts with the gas, that we need a lot of it to be sure that there are interactions a few times at least!"

In that moment, I realized that AI is the same thing.

We have discussed extensively why "artificial intelligence" is a poor choice of words; AI is no more than an engineering artifact that gives us more intelligence about some phenomena and helps automate tasks that were difficult to automate not long ago. Machine learning and autonomous, rational agents are computer scientists' and statisticians' modern microscopes. We have engineered these artifacts to help us see patterns that we otherwise would not see.

Technology—techne (the Greek word for art, craft, technique)—is a human-made device that we build and use for entering into a relationship with reality as it appears to our eyes. This reality is made up of all things in and around us: nature, ourselves, and other humans. We use technology to know the constituents of nature, to shape them, and to manipulate them.

Machine learning and robots are tools. While many speak about intelligence referring to the engineering artifact, I'd rather point out that all the intelligence still belongs to us humans! The technology is a tool that provides more intelligence to the person using the tool—it's not intelligent in itself. We wouldn't say that a liquid gas tank built to detect particles is intelligent, but like the child with her mouth and eyes filled with awe, we share this wonder for the human intelligence who created the tools that give us more intelligence about the world.

Entrepreneur and MIT Media Lab Director Joi Ito, in a conversation with President Barack Obama on AI, said:

"In the Media Lab we use the term extended intelligence." A side note specifies that "Extended intelligence is using machine learning to extend the abilities of human intelligence" (*Wired*, 2016).

ETHICS AIN'T AN ALGORITHM

As much as we struggle to make machines sentient or human-like, we don't solve the ethics of AI by trying to imbue ethical rules in machines.

When Professor Jonathan Haidt explained that only after you have a description of human beings and human morality, including all its variations, can you begin to make normative statements, he added:

"So obviously one can do simple calculations that more lives saved is better than fewer lives saved. Or, all else equal, it is right to save more lives. Still, it is almost never the case that all else is equal. Any realistic attempt to program a self-driving car would have to do so much more than just calculate lives lost in order to produce an instantiation of that fix that real human beings would find ethical."

Remaining on the example of self-driving cars, Professor Julia Stoyanovich explained the problem with the trolley dilemma in an online class on responsible AI.

An autonomous car would operate under a high degree of uncertainty in real life. For example, it would likely not know there are people in the two possible steering directions, let alone how many of them, their age, and social representation. Would it be enough to apply the famous utilitarian principle attributed to economist and moral philosopher Jeremy Bentham who reportedly said, "It is the greatest happiness of the greatest number that is the measure of right and wrong?" (Stoyanovich, 2021).

As Stoyanovich reveals, "Sounds great indeed. Unfortunately, applying these ideas to self-driving cars and the design and operation of technology more generally opens up a can of worms. And it has a name: algorithmic morality." Algorithmic morality is programming moral reasoning into algorithmic systems. This has many problems: reasoning under uncertainty, attributing responsibility, and social changes, just to name a few. Some scientists, in fact, tried it.

Wallach and Allen's book *Moral Machines: Teaching Robots Right from Wrong* (2009) recounts one of the first attempts to look into teaching moral laws to robots. It is meaningful to note that in their concluding thoughts, the authors acknowledge the real problem is about human ethical decision-making rather than machines':

"We started with the deliberately naive idea that ethical theories might be turned into decision procedures, even algorithms. But we found that top-down ethical theorizing is computationally unworkable for real-time decisions. Furthermore, the prospect of reducing ethics to a logically consistent principle or set of laws is suspect, given the complex intuitions people have about right and wrong."

A human person, as Wallach and Allen note, has intuitions about right and wrong. So, it is worth exploring what we can say about such instincts. Hence the point of view flips from teaching to the machines to teaching to humans: "In writing this book, we have learned that the process of designing (ro)bots capable of distinguishing right from wrong reveals as much about human ethical decision making as about AI."

Haidt, conversing about this subject, added: "I don't think that ethics is or can be fully rational, all the way down. So, yes. If an ethical system begins with an axiom that human lives are valuable, and it cannot justify that axiom, that's okay with me. I understand why that would bother rationalists or people who want to make every aspect of ethics explicit and perhaps programmable. But I think that might turn out to be impossible, and I'm okay with that."

The critical issue isn't "teaching" morality and ethics to machines. Instead, it's educating ourselves about ethical and moral concepts that we seem to have replaced with mere utilitarian profit-making in the business world—and to some extent, in academia.

Stoyanovich (2021) concludes that "the work of collectively understanding what's right or wrong is what roots the design of technology in people."

It is not up to the engineering artifact to make moral decisions but to the human person adopting the tool. I found it compelling visiting philosophers, educators, and spiritual leaders conveying a more encompassing vision of the human being. This is a great starting point for actively engaging in a debate on what harms and benefits different uses of AI generate.

The *Homo economicus*, the notion of the human person the economic theory proposed, is too oversimplified. It is a questionable model of the person and what drives its agency. It might be an "easier" model to accept because it spares the effort to share profound questions and ideas with others. But it is often facing the tough conversation that makes us grow into better people.

Previously, we visited the human's intuition about right and wrong, what Giussani calls the *elementary experience*—this inner longing for beauty, freedom, justice, and truth that human persons share. Comparing actions against these aspirations will help us bring the conversation of the ethics of AI to a more human level.

When I took philosophy classes in high school, my favorite philosopher was Socrates. He used to ask his interlocutors *ti esti*—what is it? He wanted to break the flow of the often abstract rhetorical discourse to get to a rational, universally accepted definition of the speech's premises. Only after having established the definitions as premises can one construct an argument.

Designing ethical technology must start by reminding ourselves and educating others about the fundamental constituents of the human person. Humane organizations must develop spaces, initiatives, and products that safeguard the essential features that make us human.

So, the ethics of AI is really about the ethics of humans. All we have learned so far, the Socratic method, and Giussani's *elementary experience* are the principles that ground my to-do list for the development of ethical AI. Before starting to code, here are my three recommendations for the creators and makers who want to design better AI products.

TI ESTI

The first point is to always define what it is that you're doing. Before getting overexcited and writing code—or asking your engineers to develop a machine learning product—ask yourself, your boss, and subordinates a few questions:

- Why are we developing this product? Define the purpose.
- Who are the users, and who are the people impacted by this product? Define the stakeholders.
- How does it work? Define how the product shall work.
- What is the impact on the persons affected by the product? Define how the product impacts a person's dimensions: relationality, freedom, transcendence.

Think about a tech company developing a recommendation engine. The purpose usually is something like increasing sales or clicks or time spent on the platform. The stakeholders would be, first and foremost, the platform's users. These are people, and so are the indirect stakeholders, like the user's relatives, communities, and relationships. The intended impact would not only be achieving the stated objective, but the side effects too. Perhaps increasing time spent on the platform harms the person's capacity for relationships. Or it harms their freedom—recommending a book, a video, or a movie influences their behavior, ideas, and actions. This is where monitoring of the feedback loop and governance plays a critical role.

THE FEEDBACK LOOP: COMPARE WITH YOUR INNER VALUES

An excellent feedback loop could be to compare our *elementary experience* with the impact analysis first, and feedback from users later: perhaps our recommender system has achieved its objective, but does its impact on people satisfy my thirst for justice, truth, beauty, etc.? Can I sleep well at night knowing with certainty that my machine learning product is doing good for its stakeholders? Again, we see a point briefly mentioned above: technology is the way we relate with reality—we shape it as well as reality shapes us through technology. What movie we watch, what book we read may change our perspectives, tastes, and ideas substantially.

Here are some recommendations:

- Before launching a product, design how all stakeholders can send you feedback, and make this process easy and convenient.
- Don't forget that the product creators are key stakeholders, too. What are their incentives?
- Have in place a process for implementing feedback, even if that means shutting down the product.
- Humans care. If you're human, show you care and mean it. Send timely and appropriate responses for every piece of feedback. Overcommunication is a good sign of building rapport—humans are relational beings. At each step of the feedback loop (stakeholder input, action, resolution), send updates, and transparent explanations, keeping everything easy-to-understand.

DATA IS PEOPLE

Finally, when treating data, don't forget that behind data, there are real persons. Like Associate Professor of the history of science at Harvard Rebecca Lemov says in an excellent essay: "Big data is people" (2016). Data privacy is an important topic that I haven't treated in this book as much as it deserves. Still, it is one of the areas in technology that we already have a good awareness of, and many regulatory frameworks protect it. However, it is worth pointing out a few questions about treating data properly:

- Do people know what data they have to trade to use the product and how the companies or products will use the data?
- Does the product cross the creepy line? For example, do you have users unpleasantly surprised about how much you know about them?
- Could a ten-year-old understand your privacy policy?
- Challenge your business model if there are any conflicts between how the product achieves the organization's objectives and how it shall use (and protect!) data.

In the recommender engine example, consider how a customer would feel if she started receiving recommendations for pregnancy products when she may not even know she is pregnant. Again, comparing with your inner values, does it feel right, just, or beautiful? Do you have the proper process in place for hearing and caring about customer feedback?

One final note would be to include as many and disparate points of view as possible across all the three points mentioned above. Haidt made a fantastic observation when we spoke:

"The internet was invented with a kind of a left libertarian ethos. In which, the thought was 'if we just connect everybody up, it'll be great and it'd be great for democracy. Let information be flowing free, and this will empower people.' So there was a kind of a left libertarian ethos.

"What if the internet had been designed with some input from conservatives? For example, social conservatives with an ethos more concerned with security. What if the internet had been designed from the beginning with better security? And a better protection of privacy, a better ability to keep out trolls and bad actors. If that had been the case, we would have a much better internet.

"I would say this thinking applies here. AI may be advancing faster than the internet ever did. Its advanced transformative effects on how we live could be far beyond those of the internet. If it is developed by engineers and mathematicians and computer scientists without input from a broad variety of fields and perspectives, then I think we will end up with an AI that has a much higher ratio of negative to positive effects."

* * *

Throughout this book, I tried to use the Socratic method: we have visited many definitions. By the end of this journey, I hope to give you a solid understanding of AI. We saw its origin, history, and development. I presented what machine learning is, the modern computer technique powering most AI applications. We visited applications that use AI and machine learning with their problems and opportunities. Entering into the ethics of AI, we have defined concepts like realism, reasonableness, and morality's impact in acquiring knowledge. Finally, we attempted to represent the constituents of the human person.

Russo and Vaccaro, in their long essay for defining a better economic model for the development of the human person as a whole, suggest that appropriate progress should safeguard and develop three critical dimensions of the human person: freedom (free action and decision making), relationality (capacity to form and nurture relationships), and transcendence (the ability to overcome limits) (Russo and Vaccaro, 2013).

When we visited the origins of AI, we noticed that not all technology breakthroughs brought real progress. We discovered that the key to real progress is investing in our ethical formation and inner growth on this journey.

Machines will not spare us this task! And I'd like to invite more and more engineers and technology developers to invest in ethical formation. It made me laugh but also worry when I read what MIT's Ito said:

"This may upset some of my students at MIT, but one of my concerns is that it's been a predominately male gang of kids, mostly white, who are building the core computer science around AI, and they're more comfortable talking to computers than to human beings. A lot of them feel that if they could just make that science fiction, generalized AI, we wouldn't have to worry about all the messy stuff like politics and society. They think machines will just figure it all out for us" (*Wired*, 2016).

A few years ago, I read a book that made me realize the driving force behind the exponential technological progress we are experiencing (Kotler and Wheal, 2017). It's humans' thirst for transcendence. We want to be godlike.

This isn't necessarily a spiritual or religious concept. We have seen how we have an inner drive for going beyond our limits. Transcendence means to transcend our limitations—to break them and reach a new standard. Then doing it all over again.

In fact, the book I mentioned draws a potent metaphor between our age and the ancient Greek myths. Its title is *Stealing Fire*—referring to the legend of titan Prometheus, who created humanity from clay, stole fire from Zeus, and donated it to humanity. In the podcast episode where Tristan Harris interviews historian Yuval Harari, all participants refer to AI technology as "godlike technology" (Harris and Raskin, 2021). Technology is viewed as the Promethean fire.

Now, "godlike" might be too far-fetched. I'm ready to bet God would be way wiser than a machine learning algorithm!

But the point remains: we want to be like God. This is the exciting quest of humanity. We build technology to break our limits, and there are different ways to overcome those limits. We can do it as a fraternity of humans, compassionate about each other and able to forgive limitations, starting with our personal ones. Or we can overpower each other and individualistically try to make it on our own. I am concerned that many people leading the technology giants today are following the latter. They realize many drawbacks, and this gives me hope, but will they have the courage to make a drastic change? Will they give up their power (Segall, 2019)?

I'd like to go for the first option. So, let's work together: you can find more essays, articles, and ways to contact me on https://amchierici.github.io.

I hope this book provided you with a different, nontrivial perspective on AI, human progress, our relationship with technology, and a starting point for being a little more moral.

Acknowledgments

A special thank you to every person who had conversations with me regarding the topics of this book, especially those who spent considerable time teaching me something valuable. In particular, I want to thank: Julia Stoyanovich, her fantastic class on responsible data science ignited my motivation for writing; Jonathan Haidt, his research in moral psychology opened up a fantastic universe I desire to dive deeper into in the following years, and his intellectual honesty should be an example for NYU and the wider academic community; and Pat Fagan, his insights and availability have been a tremendous help.

A big thank you to the team contributing to the exhibition *Humans and Machines*, the first step for gathering thoughts and material on the ethics of AI: Andrea Bellavia, Elisa Piscitelli, Francesco Nordio, Giacomo Vianello, John Paul Chiodini, Owen Kunhardt, and Peter Fields.

Thank you to all my Beta Readers: your revisions and feedback were invaluable. Special thanks to those who reviewed many chapters: Michele Curtoni, John Paul Chiodini, and Salam Khalifa.

Last but not least, a huge thank you to all the fantastic contributors to my crowdfunding campaign. You have made this publication possible:

Alessandra Pedrocchi,
Alessandra Venerus,
Alessandro Ventura,
Alessandro Vitale,
Andrea Bellavia,
Andrea Ninni,
Andrea Prestipino,
Andrea Riganti,
Andrey Vedishchev,
Andy Wright ,
Ansgar Koene,
Antonino Nicotra,
Armando Fumagalli,
Arthur Leymonie,
asala218,
Bashar Alhafni,
Bernardo Cavalleri,
Bruno Marsico,
Buscone Serena,
Buu Truong,
Carlo Torniai,
Carlos J. Henriquez,
Cathy Carroll,
Chamkaur Ghag,
Chiara Buriol,
Chiara Tamarindi,
Christian Groehe,
Christian Jan,
Claudio Magni,
Cynthia Flynn,
Davide Arrigoni,
Davide Manstretta,
Davide Mazzini,
Domenico Crapanzano,
Edward Tredger,
Eisel Chiara ,
Ekene Uzoma ,
Elisa Piscitelli,
Emilio Giulio Orsenigo,
Enea Fochesato,
Enrico De Petri,
Enrico Nardelli,
Eric Koester,
Erika McDonnell,
Esila Obiang,
Federico Da Col,
Francesca Greselin,
Francesco Maria Cerutti,
Francesco Nordio,
Francesco Arneodo,
Frederico Martins ,
Giacomo Aletti,
Giacomo Vianello,
Giorgio Bacelli,
Giulio Pepe,
Hani Majzoub,

Iain Hamilton,
Joseph E Flynn,
Joseph West,
JP Chiodini,
Juanmi Lopez,
Kertu Koss,
Larry Orimoloye,
Laura Manenti,
Laura Staccoli,
Lorenzo Chierici,
Lorenzo Rossi,
Luca Marinozzi,
luca notarangelo,
Luca Sambucci,
Luca Tizzano,
Lucia Parolini,
Marcello Capucciati,
Margherita Laffranchi,
Mariapaola Testa,
Marta Maria Perego,
Martin Lehnert,
Maryia Kavaliova,
Matteo Cerri,
Matteo Schgor,
Michele Benetti,
Michele Curtoni,
Munish Mehta,
Niall Bellabarba,
Nicola Maria Atum Salandini,
Nicola Matteucci,
Niklas Huyeng,
Nikolaos Petalas,
Paolo Maestri,
Paolo Testa,
Paolo Tognini,
pasqua Sumerano,
Pasquale Aaviano,
Patrick Fagan,
patsoredneb,
Paul Tozour,
Peter Fields,
Pietro Canal,
Pinar Emirdag,
Riccardo Manenti,
Rick Huckstep,
Robberto,
Roberto Avallone,
Salam Khalifa,
Sebastiaan Verborg,
Sebastien Tinnes ,
Shriya Mehta,
Simone Franchini,
Simonetta D'Italia Wiener,
Stefano Maria Chierici,
W M. Awad,
Wahib Kamran,
Will Newman,
Xi Chen,
XinRan Liu.

Appendix

INTRODUCTION

Baraniuk, Chris. "Artificially Intelligent Painters Invent New Styles of Art." *NewScientist*, June 29, 2017. https://www.newscientist.com/article/2139184-artificially-intelligent-painters-invent-new-styles-of-art/.

Bosker, Bianca. "The Binge Breaker: Tristan Harris Believes Silicon Valley Is Addicting Us to Our Phones. He's Determined to Make It Stop." *The Atlantic*, November 2016. https://www.theatlantic.com/magazine/archive/2016/11/the-binge-breaker/501122/.

Cellan-Jones, Rory. "Stephen Hawking Warns Artificial Intelligence Could End Mankind." *BBC*, December 2, 2014. https://www.bbc.com/news/technology-30290540.

Dizikes, Peter. "Study: On Twitter, False News Travels Faster than True Stories." *MIT News Office*, March 8, 2018. https://news.mit.edu/2018/study-twitter-false-news-travels-faster-true-stories-0308.

Pope Francis. *Laudato si*. Vatican City: Vatican Press, May 24, 2015: w2. Sec. 122.

Lucas, Louise. "Alibaba and Microsoft AI Beat Humans in Stanford Reading Test." *Financial Times*, January 15, 2018. https://www.ft.com/content/8763219a-f9bc-11e7-9b32-d7d59aace167.

Marr, Bernard. "28 Best Quotes About Artificial Intelligence." *Forbes*, July 25, 2017. https://www.forbes.com/sites/bernardmarr/2017/07/25/28-best-quotes-about-artificial-intelligence/?sh=3c91bff84a6f.

Ng, Andrew. "What Artificial Intelligence Can and Can't Do Right Now." *Harvard Business Review*, November 09, 2016. https://hbr.org/2016/11/what-artificial-intelligence-can-and-cant-do-right-now.

Ray, Amit. *Compassionate Artificial Intelligence: Frameworks and Algorithms*. Compassionate AI Lab (An Imprint of Inner Light Publishers), 2018.

Stanford Encyclopedia of Philosophy. s.v. "Relativism." Accessed May 8, 2021, https://plato.stanford.edu/entries/relativism/.

The Irish Times. "Could a Computer Think like a Human?" July 8, 1996. https://www.irishtimes.com/news/could-a-computer-think-like-a-human-1.65127.

Turing, Alan. "Intelligent Machinery, a Heretical Theory." The Turing Digital Archive. Accessed May 10, 2021. http://www.turingarchive.org/browse.php/b/4.

THE ORIGINS OF AI

Anderson, John R. *Cognitive Psychology and Its Implication*. San Francisco: W. H. Freeman, 1980.

Beckermann, Ansgar. "Darwin–What if Man is Only an Animal, After All?" *dialectica* 64, no. 4 (2010): 467–482. https://www.jstor.org/stable/24706227?seq=1.

Goodman, Nelson. *Fact, Fiction, and Forecast*. Cambridge, MA and London, England: Harvard University Press, 1983.

Harari, Yuval Noah. *Sapiens: A Brief History of Humankind*. Random House, 2014.

History.com Editors. "Atomic Bomb History." A&E Television Networks, updated February 21, 2020. https://www.history.com/topics/world-war-ii/atomic-bomb-history.

Hodson, Hal. "DeepMind and Google: The Battle to Control Artificial Intelligence." *The Economist*, March 1, 2019. https://www.economist.com/1843/2019/03/01/deepmind-and-google-the-battle-to-control-artificial-intelligence.

Kraemer, Barbara. "Development-Principles for Integral Human Development in Sollicitudo Rei Socialis." *International Journal of Social Economics* 25, no. 11/12 (December 1998): 1727–1738. https://doi.org/10.1108/03068299810233394.

O'Neill, Aaron. "Number of Unemployed Persons Worldwide from 2010 to 2019 and Projections until 2023." *Statista*, March 31, 2021. https://www.statista.com/statistics/266414/unemployed-persons-worldwide/.

Orlowski, Jeff, dir. *The Social Dilemma*. Netflix Original, 2020. https://www.netflix.com/title/81254224.

Russel, Stuart, and Peter Norvig. *Artificial Intelligence: A Modern Approach*. London: Pearson Education Limited, 2013.

Russo, Francesco, and Antonio Vaccaro. *Lo sviluppo umano integrale & le organizzazioni lavorative*. Siena: Cantagalli, 2013.

Smith, Adam. *An Inquiry into the Nature and Causes of the Wealth of Nations*. London: W. Strahan and T. Cadell, 1776.

WHAT IS ARTIFICIAL INTELLIGENCE

AeroAstroMIT. "Centennial Symposium: One-One-One with Elon Musk." October 31, 2014. Video, 1:15:32. https://aeroastro.mit.edu/videos/centennial-symposium-one-one-one-elon-musk.

Bellman, Richard. *An Introduction to Artificial Intelligence: Can Computers Think?* San Francisco: Boyd & Fraser Pub. Co., 1978.

Covington, Paul, Jay Adams, and Emre Sargin. "Deep Neural Networks for YouTube Recommendations." In Proceedings of the 10th ACM Conference on Recommender Systems, 191–198. 2016.

Dowd, Maureen. "Elon Musk, Blasting Off in Domestic Bliss." *The New York Times*, July 25, 2020. https://www.nytimes.com/2020/07/25/style/elon-musk-maureen-dowd.html.

Koumchatzky, Nicholas, and Anton Andryeyev. "Using Deep Learning at Scale in Twitter's Timelines." Twitter Blog, May 9, 2017. https://blog.twitter.com/engineering/en_us/topics/

insights/2017/using-deep-learning-at-scale-in-twitters-timelines.html.

Kurzweil, Ray. *The Age of Intelligent Machines*. Cambridge, MA: MIT Press, 1990.

Lewis, Paul. "'Fiction Is Outperforming Reality': How YouTube's Algorithm Distorts Truth." *The Guardian*, February 2, 2018. https://www.theguardian.com/technology/2018/feb/02/how-youtubes-algorithm-distorts-truth.

Merriam Webster Dictionary. s.v. "Intelligence." Accessed May 11, 2021, https://www.merriam-webster.com/dictionary/intelligence.

Metz, Cade. "Police Drones Are Starting to Think for Themselves." *The New York Times*, December 5, 2020. https://www.nytimes.com/2020/12/05/technology/police-drones.html.

MIT Technology Review. "When Science Fiction Inspires Real Technology." April 5, 2018. https://www.technologyreview.com/2018/04/05/67057/when-science-fiction-inspires-real-technology/.

Nilsson, Nils J. *Artificial Intelligence: A New Synthesis*. Burlington, MA: Morgan Kaufmann, 1998.

Ovide, Shira. "We're Still Smarter Than Computers: For Now." *The New York Times*, November 25, 2020. https://www.nytimes.com/2020/11/25/technology/ai-gpt3.html.

Pierre, Joe. "Fake News, Echo Chambers and Filter Bubbles: A Survival Guide." *Psychology Today*, November 21, 2016. https://www.

psychologytoday.com/us/blog/psych-unseen/201611/fake-news-echo-chambers-filter-bubbles-survival-guide.

Ribeiro, Marco Tulio, Sameer Singh, and Carlos Guestrin. "'Why Should I Trust You?' Explaining the Predictions of Any Classifier." In Proceedings of the 22nd ACM SIGKDD International Conference on Knowledge Discovery and Data Mining, Pp. 1135–1144. https://arxiv.org/abs/1602.04938.

Robitzski, Dan. "You Have No Idea What Artificial Intelligence Really Does: The World of AI Is Full of Hype and Deception." *Futurism*, October 16, 2018. https://futurism.com/artificial-intelligence-hype.

Russel, Stuart, and Peter Norvig. *Artificial Intelligence: A Modern Approach*. London: Pearson Education Limited, 2013.

Salleb-Aouissi, Ansaf. "Intelligent Agents, Uninformed Search." Class lecture, Artificial Intelligence (AI), Columbia University, EdX. https://www.edx.org/course/artificial-intelligence-ai.

The University of Helsinki, Reaktor Education. "Elements of AI." (website). Accessed January 25, 2020. https://course.elementsofai.com/.

Vocabulary.com. s.v. "Artificial." Accessed May 11, 2021, https://www.vocabulary.com/dictionary/artificial.

Winston, Patrick Henry. *Artificial Intelligence* (Third edition). Reading, MA: Addison-Wesley, 1992.

MACHINE AND HUMAN LEARNING

Bahai Writings. "The Four Methods of Acquiring Knowledge." Bahai Teachings (website). February 8, 2013. https://bahaiteachings.org/the-four-methods-of-acquiring-knowledge.

BBC Studios. "Why Learning Like Humans Is So Difficult For Machines." October 1, 2015. Video, 4:14. https://youtu.be/32K-TKXZZ-BI.

DeepMind. "AlphaGo." Research, Case Studies (website). Accessed May 13, 2021. https://deepmind.com/research/case-studies/alphago-the-story-so-far.

Duhigg, Charles. "How Companies Learn Your Secrets." *The New York Times Magazine,* February 16, 2012. https://www.nytimes.com/2012/02/19/magazine/shopping-habits.html.

Merriam Webster Dictionary. s.v. "Learn." Accessed May 13, 2021, https://www.merriam-webster.com/dictionary/learn.

Merriam Webster Dictionary. s.v. "Machine." Accessed May 13, 2021, https://www.merriam-webster.com/dictionary/machine.

Naveed, Fakhar. "Various Methods of Obtaining Knowledge." Mass Communication Talk (website), September 10, 2012. https://www.masscommunicationtalk.com/various-methods-of-obtaining-knowledge.html.

Price, P. C., R. S. Jhangiani, I. A. Chiang, D. C. Leighton, and C. Cuttler. *Research Methods in Psychology (3rd American Edition).* Pullman: WSU, 2017. https://opentext.wsu.edu/carriecuttler/chapter/methods-of-knowing.

The University of Helsinki, Reaktor Education. "Elements of AI." (website). Accessed January 25, 2020. https://course.elementsofai.com/.

LIMITATIONS OF AI

Box, George E.P., and Gwilym M. Jenkins. *Time Series Analysis: Forecasting and Control*. San Francisco, CA: Holden-Day, 1976.

Brandon, John. "Terrifying High-Tech Porn: Creepy 'Deepfake' Videos Are on the Rise." *Fox News*, last updated February 20, 2018. https://www.foxnews.com/tech/terrifying-high-tech-porn-creepy-deepfake-videos-are-on-the-rise.

Devlin, Jacob, Ming-Wei Chang, Kenton Lee, and Kristina Toutanova. "BERT: Pre-training of Deep Bidirectional Transformers for Language Understanding." *arXiv preprint arXiv:1810.04805* (2018). https://arxiv.org/abs/1810.04805.

Eliot, Thomas Stearns. *The Rock*. Faber & Faber Limited, 1934.

Fedus, William, Barret Zoph, and Noam Shazeer. "Switch Transformers: Scaling to Trillion Parameter Models with Simple and Efficient Sparsity." *arXiv preprint arXiv:2101.03961* (2021). https://arxiv.org/pdf/2101.03961.pdf.

Ha, David. "Reinforcement Learning for Improving Agent Design." *Artificial Life* 25, no. 4 (2019): 352–365. https://arxiv.org/abs/1810.03779. Github repository: https://designrl.github.io/.

Hedström, Anna, Kirill Bykov, Philine Lou Bommer, Dennis Grinwald, Marina Marie-Claire Höhne. "NeurIPS 2020: Review on

Explainable AI (XAI)." *Understandable Machine Intelligence Lab* (blog), December 16, 2020. https://umilab.medium.com/neurips-2020-review-on-explainable-ai-xai-5de76381bf43.

Islam, Mo. "NeurIPS 2019: Entering the Golden Age of NLP". *Threshold Ventures* (blog), December 14, 2019. https://medium.com/threshold-ventures/neurips-2019-entering-the-golden-age-of-nlp-c8f8e4116f9d.

Metz, Cade. "Riding Out Quarantine with a Chatbot Friend: 'I Feel Very Connected.'" *The New York Times*, June 16, 2020. https://www.nytimes.com/2020/06/16/technology/chatbots-quarantine-coronavirus.html.

Morvillo, Candida. "Replika, L'app Di Intelligenza Artificiale Che Mi Ha Convinto a Uccidere Tre Persone." *Corriere Della Sera*, September 30, 2020. https://www.corriere.it/cronache/20_settembre_30/replika-l-app-intelligenza-artificiale-che-mi-ha-convinto-uccidere-tre-persone-fad86624-0285-11eb-a582-994e7abe3a15.shtml.

Murphy, Mike, and Jacob Templin. "This App Is Trying to Replicate You." Machines with Brains (Website). Accessed May 14, 2021. https://classic.qz.com/machines-with-brains/1018126/lukas-replika-chatbot-creates-a-digital-representation-of-you-the-more-you-interact-with-it/.

Price, Rob. "Microsoft Is Deleting Its AI Chatbot's Incredibly Racist Tweets". *Business Insider*, March 24, 2016. Distributed by the Internet Archive Wayback Machine. https://web.archive.org/web/20190130071430/https://www.businessinsider.com/

microsoft-deletes-racist-genocidal-tweets-from-ai-chatbot-tay-2016-3.

Rogers, Anna, Olga Kovaleva, and Anna Rumshisky. "A Primer in BERTology: What We Know about How BERT Works." *Transactions of the Association for Computational Linguistics* 8 (2020): 842-866. https://arxiv.org/pdf/2002.12327v1.pdf.

Rowley, Jennifer. "The Wisdom Hierarchy: Representations of the DIKW Hierarchy." *Journal of Information and Communication Science*, 2007. https://api.semanticscholar.org/CorpusID:17000089.

Sambucci, Luca. "Replika Mi Ha Incoraggiato a Suicidarmi (Senza Rendersene Conto)." *Notizie.AI*(blog), October 9, 2020. https://www.notizie.ai/replika-mi-ha-incoraggiato-a-suicidarmi-senza-rendersene-conto/.

Shane, Janelle. "Janelle Shane: The Danger of AI Is Weirder Than You Think." Filmed April 2019 at an Official TED conference. TED video, 10:20. https://www.ted.com/talks/janelle_shane_the_danger_of_ai_is_weirder_than_you_think.

Vincent, James. "Twitter Taught Microsoft's AI Chatbot to Be a Racist Asshole in Less than a Day." *The Verge*, March 24, 2016. https://www.theverge.com/2016/3/24/11297050/tay-microsoft-chatbot-racist.

AI, FROM FICTION TO BEHAVIORAL SCIENCE

Bernays, Edward. *Propaganda.* New York: Ig Publishing, 2005. Originally published: New York: H. Liveright, 1928.

Bock, Laszlo. *Work Rules! Insights From Inside Google That Will Transform How You Live and Lead.*Twelve, 2015.

Boyle, Danny, dir. *Steve Jobs.* UK, USA: Universal Pictures, 2015.

Burgmer, Pascal, and Birte Englich. "Bullseye! How Power Improves Motor Performance." Social Psychological and Personality Science 4, No. 2, 2013. https://doi.org/10.1177/1948550612452014.

Chu, Ben. "Father of 'Nudge Theory' Richard Thaler Wins 2017 Nobel Prize in Economics." *The Guardian*, October 9, 2017. https://www.independent.co.uk/news/business/news/richard-thaler-nobel-prize-economics-winner-2017-behavioural-economics-nudge-theory-a7990291.html.

Garland, Alex, dir. *Ex Machina.* United States: A24, 2014.

Internet Live Stats. "Twitter Usage Statistics." Accessed December 3, 2020. https://www.internetlivestats.com/twitter-statistics/.

Sweney, Mark. "How Meerkat Aleksandr Orlov Helped Increase the Market for TV Ads." *The Guardian*, January 16, 2010. https://www.theguardian.com/media/2010/jan/16/aleksander-orlov-price-comparison-ads.

Google Talks. "Decoding Clothing." December 10, 2019. Video, 45:58. https://www.youtube.com/watch?v=ooM8dLkS8oU

Ro, Christine. "The Theory of Dunbar's Number Holds That We Can Only Really Maintain about 150 Connections at Once. But Is the Rule True in Today's World of Social Media?" *BBC*, October 9, 2019. https://www.bbc.com/future/article/20191001-dunbars-number-why-we-can-only-maintain-150-relationships.

Scott, Ridley, dir. *Blade Runner.* United States: Warner Bros, 1982.

Spielberg, Steven, dir. *Ready Player One.* United States: Warner Bros, 2018.

Stanton, Andrew, Jim Morris, John Lasseter, Jim Reardon, Pete Docter, Thomas Newman, Ralph Eggleston, et al. *WALL-E.* 2008.

The New York Times. "Edward Bernays, 'Father of Public Relations' and Leader in Opinion Making, Dies at 103." March 10, 1995. https://archive.nytimes.com/www.nytimes.com/books/98/08/16/specials/bernays-obit.html.

Wachowski, Lana, and Lilly Wachowski, dir. *The Matrix.* United States: Warner Bros, 1999.

Wachowski, Lana, and Lilly Wachowski, dir. *The Matrix Reloaded.* United States: Warner Bros, 2003.

CASE STUDIES

Angwin, Julia, Jeff Larson, Surya Mattu, and Lauren Kirchner. "Machine Bias: There's Software Used across the Country to Predict Future Criminals. And It's Biased against Blacks."

ProPublica, May 23, 2016. https://www.propublica.org/article/machine-bias-risk-assessments-in-criminal-sentencing.

Bogen, Miranda, and Aaron Rieke. "Help Wanted: An Examination of Hiring Algorithms, Equity, and Bias." *Upturn*, December, 2018. https://www.upturn.org/reports/2018/hiring-algorithms/.

CDC. "Road Traffic Injuries and Deaths—A Global Problem." Accessed May 19, 2021. https://www.cdc.gov/injury/features/global-road-safety/index.html

Centre for Data Ethics and Innovation. "Review into Bias in Algorithmic Decision-Making." Gov.uk. November 27, 2020. https://www.gov.uk/government/publications/cdei-publishes-review-into-bias-in-algorithmic-decision-making/main-report-cdei-review-into-bias-in-algorithmic-decision-making.

Chen, Angela, and Karen Hao. "Emotion AI Researchers Say Overblown Claims Give Their Work a Bad Name." *MIT Technology Review*, February 14, 2020. https://www.technologyreview.com/2020/02/14/844765/ai-emotion-recognition-affective-computing-hirevue-regulation-ethics/.

Dastin, Jeffrey. "Amazon Scraps Secret AI Recruiting Tool That Showed Bias Against Women." *Reuters*, October 11, 2018. https://www.reuters.com/article/us-amazon-com-jobs-automation-insight-idUSKCN1MK08G.

Denick, Lina, Arne Hintz, Joanna Redden, and Harry Warne. "Data Scores as Governance: Investigating Uses of Citizen Scoring in Public Services." Data Justice Lab, Cardiff University.

December 2018. https://datajustice.files.wordpress.com/2018/12/data-scores-as-governance-project-report2.pdf.

DiPietro, Louis. "Are Hiring Algorithms Fair? They're Too Opaque to Tell." *Cornell Chronicle*, November 20, 2019. https://news.cornell.edu/stories/2019/11/are-hiring-algorithms-fair-theyre-too-opaque-tell-study-finds.

Foot, Philippa. "The Problem of Abortion and the Doctrine of the Double Effect." *Oxford Review*, Number 5, 1967. https://philpapers.org/archive/footpo-2.pdf.

ICO. Information Commissioner's Office. "Guidance On AI and Data Protection." Accessed May 19, 2021. https://ico.org.uk/for-organisations/guide-to-data-protection/key-data-protection-themes/guidance-on-ai-and-data-protection/.

Knowledge@Wharton and Apoorv Saxena. "What's Behind JPMorgan Chase's Big Bet on Artificial Intelligence?" February 06, 2019. Produced by *Knowledge@Wharton*. Podcast, 21:40. https://knowledge.wharton.upenn.edu/article/whats-behind-jpmorgan-chases-big-bet-artificial-intelligence/.

JPMorgan Chase & Co. "Artificial Intelligence Research: Research Agenda." Accessed May 19, 2021. https://www.jpmorgan.com/technology/artificial-intelligence/research-agenda.

Harwell, Drew. "A Face-Scanning Algorithm Increasingly Decides Whether You Deserve the Job: HireVue Claims It Uses Artificial Intelligence to Decide Who's Best for a Job. Outside Experts Call It 'Profoundly Disturbing.'" *The Washington Post*, November 6, 2019. https://www.washingtonpost.com/

technology/2019/10/22/ai-hiring-face-scanning-algorithm-increasingly-decides-whether-you-deserve-job/.

Hawkins, Andrew J. "Tesla's 'Full Self-Driving' Software Is Starting to Roll Out to Select Customers." *The Verge*, October 21, 2020. https://www.theverge.com/2020/10/21/21527577/tesla-full-self-driving-autopilot-beta-software-update.

Leslie, D., L. Holmes, C. Hitrova, and E. Ott. "Ethics Review of Machine Learning in Children's Social Care." The Alan Turing Institute, January 2020. https://whatworks-csc.org.uk/wp-content/uploads/WWCSC_Ethics_of_Machine_Learning_in_CSC_Jan2020.pdf.

Logan, Bryan. "Tesla Made Autopilot a Standard Feature on All Its Vehicles and Announced Sweeping Changes to the Model 3 Lineup." *Business Insider,* April 12, 2019. https://www.businessinsider.com/tesla-model-3-lineup-changes-autopilot-comes-standard-2019-4.

Madrigal, Alexis C. "7 Arguments against the Autonomous-Vehicle Utopia: All the Ways the Self-Driving Future Won't Come to Pass." *The Atlantic*, December 20, 2018. https://www.theatlantic.com/technology/archive/2018/12/7-arguments-against-the-autonomous-vehicle-utopia/578638/.

Marsh, Sarah, and Niamh McIntyre. "Nearly Half of Councils in Great Britain Use Algorithms to Help Make Claims Decisions." *The Guardian*, October 28, 2020. https://www.theguardian.com/society/2020/oct/28/nearly-half-of-councils-in-great-britain-use-algorithms-to-help-make-claims-decisions.

Stoyanovich, Julia, Bill Howe, and H. V. Jagadish. "Responsible Data Management." *Proceedings of the VLDB Endowment* 13, no. 12 (2020): 3474–3488. https://doi.org/10.14778/3415478.3415570.

Tesla, Inc. "Tesla Vehicle Safety Report." Accessed March 3, 2021. https://www.tesla.com/en_AE/VehicleSafetyReport.

Wachowski, Lana, and Lilly Wachowski, dir. *The Matrix Reloaded*. United States: Warner Bros, 2003.

WHO. "Road Traffic Injuries." February 7, 2020. https://www.who.int/news-room/fact-sheets/detail/road-traffic-injuries.

WHAT SHOULD AI ETHICS FOCUS ON?

ACL 2019. "Program: Invited Talks." Accessed November 25, 2020. https://acl2019.org/EN/program.xhtml.html.

CAiRE. "I'm CAiRE, the Empathetic Neural Chatbot." Accessed January 18, 2021 and May 20, 2021. https://demo.caire.ust.hk/chatbot/.

China State Council. "Notice of the State Council Issuing the New Generation of Artificial Intelligence Development Plan." July 8, 2017. English Document *by The Foundation for Law and International Affairs*. https://flia.org/wp-content/uploads/2017/07/A-New-Generation-of-Artificial-Intelligence-Development-Plan-1.pdf.

Dafoe, Allan. "AI Governance: Opportunity and Theory of Impact." Allan Dafoe (website), September 2020. https://www.allandafoe.com/opportunity.

Fudano, Jun. "Why is Engineering Ethics a Current Focus of Attention?" Class lecture, Science, Engineering, AI & Data Ethics, Tokyo Institute of Technology, EdX. Accessed October 2020. https://www.edx.org/course/science-and-engineering-ethics-2.

Heaven, Will Douglas. "Predictive Policing Algorithms Are Racist. They Need to Be Dismantled." MIT Technology Review, July 17, 2020. https://www.technologyreview.com/2020/07/17/1005396/predictive-policing-algorithms-racist-dismantled-machine-learning-bias-criminal-justice/.

James, William. *The Will to Believe, Human Immortality, and Other Essays in Popular Philosophy.* New York: Dover Publications, 1956.

Jenkins, Scotty. "David Hume and Deriving an 'Ought' from an 'Is'." *The Ought*, July 10, 2017. https://theought.com/2017/07/10/david-hume-and-deriving-an-ought-from-an-is/.

Lee, Kai-Fu. "The Art of AI: Kai-Fu Lee Interviewed by Project Syndicate." *Project Syndicate*, May 29, 2020. https://www.project-syndicate.org/onpoint/state-of-ai-by-kai-fu-lee-2020-05.

Molteni, Megane. "The Chatbot Therapist Will See You Now." *Wired*, June 7, 2017. https://www.wired.com/2017/06/facebook-messenger-woebot-chatbot-therapist/.

Radclyffe, Charles, and Richard Nodell. "Ethical by Design: Measuring and Managing Digital Ethics in the Enterprise." SocArXiv. January 28, 2020. https://doi.org/10.31235/osf.io/gj2kf.

Schwartz, John. "Giving Web a Memory Cost Its Users Privacy." *The New York Times*, September 4, 2001. https://www.nytimes.com/2001/09/04/business/giving-web-a-memory-cost-its-users-privacy.html.

UnBias (website). Accessed November 20, 2020. https://unbias.wp.horizon.ac.uk.

Wired. "The President in Conversation with MIT's Joi Ito and WIRED's Scott Dadich." August 24, 2016. https://www.wired.com/2016/10/president-obama-mit-joi-ito-interview/.

WHAT IS HUMAN: PART I

Dreyfus, Hubert, and Stuart E. Dreyfus. *Mind over Machine: The Power of Human Intuition and Expertise in the Era of the Computer.* New York: Free Press, 1986.

Dreyfus, Hubert. *What Computers Still Can't Do: A Critique of Artificial Reason.* Cambridge: The MIT Press; Revised ed. (October 30, 1992), First Published in 1972.

Harari, Yuval Noah. *Homo Deus: A Brief History of Tomorrow.* New York: Harper Perennial, 2018.

Harari, Yuval Noah. *Sapiens: A Brief History of Humankind.* Random House, 2014.

Haugeland, John. "Understanding Natural Language." In *Having Thought.* Cambridge, MA: Harvard University Press. Reprinted from Journal of Philosophy, 76 (11), 619–632, 1979.

Haugeland, John. *Artificial Intelligence: The Very Idea.* Cambridge: MIT press, 1989.

Heisenberg, Werner. *Physics and Philosophy: The Revolution in Modern Science.* New York: Harper Collins Publishers Inc., 2007.

McCormick, Ken. "An Essay on the Origin of the Rational Utility Maximization Hypothesis and a Suggested Modification." *Eastern Economic Journal*, Vol. 23, No. 1, Winter, 1997. https://www.jstor.org/stable/pdf/40325751.pdf.

Stigler, George J. *The Theory of Price.* New York: Macmillan Publishing Company, 1987.

Potts, Richard, and Christopher Sloan, authors of *What Does it Mean to Be Human?* Washington, D.C.: National Geographic, 2010.

The New York Times. "Truth Headline Poster." Accessed May 28, 2021. https://store.nytimes.com/products/truth-headline-poster?variant=12180187381830.

WHAT IS HUMAN: PART II
Austen, Jane. *Mansfield Park.* Penguin Classics, 2003.

Giussani, Luigi. *The Religious Sense.* Montreal: McGill-Queen's University Press, 1997.

Haidt, Jonathan. "The New Synthesis in Moral Psychology." *Science* 316, no. 5827 (2007): 998–1002. https://science.sciencemag.org/content/316/5827/998.

Russo, Francesco, and Antonio Vaccaro. *Lo Sviluppo Umano Integrale & Le Organizzazioni Lavorative*. Siena: Cantagalli, 2013.

Sokolowski, Robert. *Phenomenology of the Human Person*. Cambridge: Cambridge University Press, 2008.

ETHICAL AI OR ETHICAL HUMANS?

Pope Benedict XVI. *Spe Salvi*. San Francisco: Ignatius Press, 2008. Sec. 22.

Harris, Tristan and Aza Raskin. "Two Million Years in Two Hours: A Conversation with Yuval Noah Harari." January 15, 2021. In *Your Undivided Attention*. Produced by Center for Humane Technology. Podcast, MP3 audio, 01:59:48. https://www.humanetech.com/podcast/28-two-million-years-in-two-hours-a-conversation-with-yuval-noah-harari.

Kotler, Steven, and Jamie Wheal. *Stealing fire: How Silicon Valley, the Navy SEALs, and maverick scientists are revolutionizing the way we live and work*. HarperCollins, 2017.

Lemov, Rebecca. "'Big Data Is People!'" *Aeon*, June 16, 2016. https://aeon.co/essays/why-big-data-is-actually-small-personal-and-very-human.

Russo, Francesco, and Antonio Vaccaro. *Lo sviluppo umano integrale & le organizzazioni lavorative*. Siena: Cantagalli, 2013.

Segall, Laurie. "6 Tech Leaders on What They Fear the Most." *Time*, January 17, 2019. https://time.com/5505456/6-things-tech-world-leaders-fear/.

Stoyanovich, Julia. "The Problems with the Trolley Problem." *We are AI*. Accessed June 14, 2021. https://dataresponsibly.github.io/we-are-ai/modules/who-lives-who-dies-who-decides/the-problem/.

Wallach, Wendell, and Colin Allen. *Moral Machines: Teaching Robots Right from Wrong.* Oxford: Oxford University Press, 2009.

Wired. "The President in Conversation with MIT's Joi Ito and WIRED's Scott Dadich." August 24, 2016. https://www.wired.com/2016/10/president-obama-mit-joi-ito-interview/.

ENDNOTES

1. The Turing Test involves an interrogator who speaks with an agent via a screen. He doesn't know whether the answers he gets are generated by a person or a computer. Suppose the interrogator cannot tell the difference. In that case, the computer agent passes the test, and it can be classified as artificial intelligence. This test was developed by Alan Turing, the father of computing, in 1950. Today we know well that a computer can pass this test with relative ease by merely applying simple rules and well-scripted answers without truly understanding the interrogator's questions.

2. ADS may include systems not using AI.

3. CRM (Customer Relationship Management) are software tools usually adopted by salespeople. They use many machine learning techniques to analyze conversations with a sales prospect, demographics, and business data points to predict probabilities for closing a deal. In recruiting, the candidate is the deal to close for the headhunter.

4   An Institutional Review Board (IRB) is an administrative body established by universities to protect the rights and welfare of human research subjects recruited to participate in research activities conducted under the auspices of the institution with which it is affiliated.

www.ingramcontent.com/pod-product-compliance
Lightning Source LLC
LaVergne TN
LVHW012100070526
838200LV00074BA/3819